A Place for *Wonder*

A Place for *Wonder*

Reading and Writing Nonfiction in the Primary Grades

Georgia Heard & Jennifer McDonough

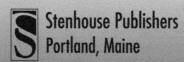

Stenhouse Publishers
Portland, Maine

Stenhouse Publishers
www.stenhouse.com

Credits
Pages 2–3: "Straight Lines" by Georgia Heard appears by permission of the author.
Page 71: "Stars" by Georgia Heard, from *Star Magic*, edited by Lee Bennett Hopkins. Copyright © 2009. Reprinted by permission of the author.
Page 80: "Will We Ever See?" from *Creatures of Earth, Sea, and Sky: Animal Poems* by Georgia Heard. Copyright © 1992. Reprinted by permission of the author.

Library of Congress Cataloging-in-Publication Data
Heard, Georgia.
  A place for wonder : reading and writing nonfiction in the primary grades / Georgia Heard and Jennifer McDonough.
     p. cm.
  Includes bibliographical references.
  ISBN 978-1-57110-432-8 (alk. paper)
  1. English language--Composition and exercises--Study and teaching (Primary)--United States. 2. Reading (Primary)--United States. 3. Active learning--United States. 4. Nature study--Activity programs--United States. I. McDonough, Jennifer, 1974- II. Title.
  LB1529.U5H43 2009
  372.64--dc22

                                                                                    2009020042

Cover design, interior design, and typesetting by Designboy Creative Group

Manufactured in the United States of America

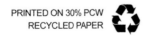
PRINTED ON 30% PCW
RECYCLED PAPER

15 14   9 8 7 6

Georgia: For Dermot and Leo—for the wonder of it all

Jen: For Brian, my amazing husband, and for Will,
who helps me see the world with wondering eyes

Contents

Chapter Three: **Nonfiction Research Wonder Writing**..79

Acknowledgments

When the poet Wislawa Szymborska gave her Nobel Prize acceptance speech she said, "I value that little phrase 'I don't know' so highly. It's small, but it flies on mighty wings." We began *A Place for Wonder: Reading and Writing Nonfiction in the Primary Classroom* with that same small but mighty phrase, "I don't know." We knew we wanted to design a thinking, creative, wonder-filled environment where kids' questions fueled their learning and was a by-product of their wondering. But we didn't know what a "wonder" classroom would look like. We didn't know how the children's enthusiasm for learning would change. Just as the students' "I don't knows" were the wings that flew their inspiration, our "I don't knows" transformed us.

In any community, there are those who stand beside us, holding our hands, telling us to take our time, and trusting our instincts and explorations. We'd like to give thanks to them.

We first thank our wonderful editor and friend, Bill Varner, who waited patiently; through steadfast and intelligent conversations over the years, our "I don't knows" slowly transformed into this book. Thanks also to Chris Downey and Jay Kilburn, for their dedicated and inspired work on the design and production; Toby Gordon, for her brilliant title brainstorm; and, as always, Philippa Stratton and Tom Seavey, who continue to guide me, and many authors, with their brilliance and exemplary insights.

We also want to give our heartfelt thanks to Karen Basil, the curriculum coordinator and upper-grade literacy coach at the Benjamin School, and Robyn Quaid, the head of Lower School at the Benjamin School, two brilliant women whose thoughtful leadership and inspiring friendship have guided us throughout this project.

Thanks also to our colleagues who continue to inspire us with their work on nonfiction: Lucy Calkins, Kathy Collins, Ralph Fletcher, Steph Harvey, Debbie Miller, JoAnn Portalupi, and Tony Stead, among others.

Georgia:

First, I would like to thank my friend, colleague, and coauthor, Jen McDonough, for her wise teaching, and for the opportunity to have reflective conversations over the past few years that have been a joy and an inspiration that resulted in our book. I also want to give thanks to the teachers at the Benjamin School for their tireless work and exceptional guidance on behalf of all the children but particularly my son who has flourished at the school. Special thanks to Franki Sibberson and Jen Allen, for their helpful comments on a draft that pushed our thinking and encouraged us at just the right moment. Thanks to Mrs. Buck in Canada and all the teachers who wrote to me with examples and thoughts after attending my nonfiction wonder workshops. And finally, as always, I'm grateful to my husband, Dermot, and our son, Leo, for their constant support and love.

Jen:

I thank Georgia, first, for inspiring me to be not only a better teacher but also a better person—the kind of person who strives for more wisdom and searches for answers. I will be forever grateful for the opportunities she provided for me both personally and professionally. Thanks to my team: Megan Kascak, Tara Hughes, Kristin Ackerman, Krista Monahan, and Jessica Eriksen, who push me to grow while keeping me grounded. To the associate teachers who work with us every day, the unsung heroes who allow us to grow the way we do, thank you! To the two wonderful teachers with whom I share a classroom, Audra Cato and Peg Meehan, you amazing women are always there for me offering enduring support! Thanks for "going with the flow!" To all of the Benjamin School "family," you have been the ones to watch me grow as a teacher. Thanks for all of the openness and sharing. Sherri Danyali and Dr. Jill Jones, you both taught me to say, "Why not?" instead of "Why?" It made me believe I could run 10Ks and be a writer. To my best friend, Tiffany Turner, who is always on the other end of the phone no matter what. I have never once talked to you without laughter—you know me better than anyone. Thanks for helping me get through the stressful stuff! Mom, Dad, Kate, and Abby, thanks for putting up with me and believing in me the way you do. You gave me the confidence to go out into the world and achieve what I have. The McDonoughs who are always there to say, "Way to go!" And, of course, Brian and Will. Our family hug is what keeps me going, I love you guys.

To see a world in a grain of sand,
And a heaven in a wildflower,
Hold infinity in the palm of your hand,
And eternity in an hour.

~ William Blake

Introduction

When my son was three, we wandered down our street together looking for treasures. It took a half hour to walk two steps as he stopped to pick up a rock, gaze at a ladybug, cradle a seedling from a banyan tree, or stuff a lizard's egg into his pocket. By the end of the walk, his pockets were filled with these treasures. My son was doing what all young children do: they see the extraordinary in the ordinary; they see the beauty in the ugly; they see the magic in the small, where many adults are too busy to notice.

Lewis Thomas writes in his book *Late Night Thoughts on Listening to Mahler's Ninth Symphony* (1983):

> *The word wonder comes from the ancient Indo-European root meaning simply to smile or to laugh. Anything wonderful is something to smile in the presence of. (56)*

When my son set off to kindergarten, I hoped that school would nurture his sense of wonder, make him smile and laugh each day, fuel his desire to explore the world, and spark his imagination just as our walks and exploration time had done at home.

I observed a class of kindergarten children returning from recess. I was alarmed at what I saw and wrote "Straight Lines" to express how I felt (a reproducible version is included in the Appendix).

Straight Lines

> *All the kindergartners*
> *walk to recess and back*
> *in a perfectly straight line*
> *no words between them.*
> *They must stifle their small voices,*
> *their laughter, they must*
> *stop the little skip in their walk,*
> *they must not dance or hop*
> *or run or exclaim.*
> *They must line up*

at the water fountain
straight, and in perfect form,
like the brick wall behind them.
One of their own given the job
of informer — guard of quiet,
soldier of stillness.
If they talk
or make a sound
they will lose their stars.
Little soldiers marching to and from
pretend
their hair sweaty
from escaping dinosaurs
their hearts full of loving the world
and all they want to do
is shout it out
at the top of their lungs.
When they walk back to class
they must quietly
fold their pretends into pockets,
must dam the river of words,
ones they're just learning
new words that hold the power
to light the skies, and if they don't
a star is taken away.
One star
by one star
until night grows dark and heavy
while they learn to think carefully
before skipping,
before making a wish.

What bothered me was not the no-talking rule—it was deeper and more systemic than that; it was about watching young children's enthusiasm, wonder, and freedom trained out of them.

Many primary classrooms are now teaching to a test in classrooms where opportunities for curiosity, creativity, and exploration are rare. Some schools have become places where learning to line up quietly is what the school values: such values as a silent class instead of students engaged in meaningful conversation, learning to take a test instead of discovering and asking questions, sitting silently at a desk all day preparing for a test. In other words, many elementary schools are valuing "straight lines" in both behavior and thought.

A principal of an elementary school in Florida thought that practicing for the state test, the Florida Comprehensive Assessment Test (FCAT), would give kindergarten students an advantage. They wanted to call the kindergarten practice test the FKITTY. One Florida mother told me that because of testing, her son's kindergarten class reduced recess to five minutes. A letter came home explaining the new set of rules for recess: only one time down the slide and only one swing on the swing set.

What's happened to education in which our youngest students are forced to practice for a test at the exclusion of play, curiosity, and exploration? Tests can't measure the essential habits and understandings of young children that will make them lifelong learners.

As we read a myriad of state standards, we noticed a discordance between what tests measure and what standards recommend. We discovered that although most tests measure finite skills, many primary-grade state standards encourage teaching for understanding, critical thinking, creativity, and question asking, and promote the development of children who have the attributes of inventiveness, curiosity, engagement, imagination, and creativity.

For example, a Pennsylvania standard for kindergarten states that "the learning environment for young children [should] stimulate and engage their curiosity about the world around them" as well as "enhance their curiosity and knowledge about the world in which they live in" (Pennsylvania Department of Education and Department of Public Welfare 2007, 7-9).

Several other states' standards affirm that children should:

- Demonstrate initiative and curiosity
- Demonstrate growing eagerness and satisfaction to discover and discuss a growing range of topics, ideas, and tasks
- Use multiple strategies and all available senses to explore and learn from the environment

Many state standards recognize the importance of setting up classroom environments that encourage discovery and curiosity. We compiled a list of the standards and curriculum points that connect to the work in this book.

- Stimulate curiosity

- Learn through inquiry and observation

- Recognize and solve problems through observation, active exploration, interactions, and discussions with peers and adults

- Gather data through senses

- Stimulate imagination and creativity

- Respond with wonderment and awe

- Find or determine answers to questions derived from curiosity about everyday experiences

These are the habits that will last a lifetime and help develop intelligent, alive human beings who value the beauty of the planet, are fascinated and interested in the world, and ask questions and live a life connected to other people and the global community.

Matthew Fox writes that we are in need of "wisdom schools," as opposed to "knowledge factories." "A wisdom school would honor the heart and body, the right brain of awe and wonder. . . . We must educate about awe—awe of our universe, awe of our planet and its eighteen-billion-year story, awe of the creatures with whom we share this planet" (1995, 170, 173).

We were fortunate because my son's kindergarten teacher, Jen McDonough, and other teachers at his school shared similar goals and concerns, and we began to work together to create primary classrooms filled with wonder.

We envisioned this book first as a menu of centers, projects, and ideas that teachers can weave into already existing curriculums and that will help teachers create a classroom of thinking, questioning, and discovering. Second, we envisioned this book as a new way to approach a nonfiction unit of study that embraces our belief that purposeful and authentic writing and reading come from children's own authentic and passionate wonders and observations about their world.

Since beginning this book, we've noticed a wave of other books that touch on and support our thinking about creating environments at home and in the world that provide time and opportunities for discovery and wonder. The most popular of these books is *The Last Child in the Woods: Saving Our Children from Nature Deficit Disorder* by Richard Louv (2008), which describes the alienation many children feel toward nature and the consequences of that alienation. Louv also started the Children & Nature Network Web site, which is designed to build a movement that helps children reconnect with nature. The professional book *Childhood and Nature: Design Principles for Educators* by David T. Sobel (2008) makes the case that meaningful connections with the natural world don't begin in the rain forest but in our own backyards and communities. And *Schoolyard-Enhanced Learning: Using the Outdoors as an Instructional Tool, K-8* by Herbert W. Broda (2007) shows how the school grounds, whether your school is in an urban, a suburban, or a rural setting, can become an enriching extension of the classroom. Whether kids live in New York City or other urban areas or in the middle of rural Iowa, helping children reconnect with the natural world sparks wonder and curiosity.

Together, Jen and I pondered about creating a wonder environment. Our goal was to create a landscape of wonder in primary classrooms—a landscape in children's minds and hearts filled with wonder and awe about this amazing world we live in.

We were delightfully surprised with the way the children evolved in their thinking. Those end-of-the-day glassy-eyed looks of yesterday were replaced by ferocious curiosity.

We urge you to give the ideas presented here a try, even if it feels different at first. Build this new feeling of wonderment into a habit of mind. Your children and your classroom will change. There will be energy you never imagined. Some days may feel unorganized and unproductive, especially in the beginning, but we think you'll come to see that it's worthwhile.

Chapter One

Creating a Wonder World:
Centers, Projects, and Clubs

*It is more important to pave the way for the child to want to know
than to put him on a diet of facts he is not ready to assimilate.*

~ *Rachel Carson*

Introduction

Recently, I had the pleasure of listening to my friend and colleague Ralph Fletcher give a writing seminar. He asked us to draw a map of an outdoor place where we spent time in our childhoods: backyards, streets, vacant lots, woods. He then asked us to mark an *X* on a spot that evoked a sense of wonder and mystery. I drew a map of my backyard in Virginia. I marked an *X* on the small creek that meandered behind our house — I spent many hours of wonder there — a place where king snakes slithered next to our Keds-covered feet, and crayfish peered at us from under the rocks where they lurked.

As I was driving home, I thought about why so many of our schools and classrooms aren't places of wonder. If we asked children to make a map of their classrooms, and then mark an *X* on a place they feel is a wonder spot, a place where they are excited to learn and to explore, a place where they can discover new things, where would that place be? The classroom library? Sitting next to the fish tank on the shelf? Rummaging through the art box filled with colored markers and paper? We need to think about creating primary classroom environments that give children the opportunity for wonder, mystery, and discovery; an environment that speaks to young children's inherent curiosity and innate yearning for exploration is a classroom where children are passionate about learning and love school.

I remember once visiting a first-grade classroom in New York City where the sense of wonder was evident everywhere. If I were to draw an *X* on the places in this classroom where I would want to explore, investigate, and learn, my entire map would be covered with *X*s. The teacher had propped a spring cherry tree branch in full bloom in a corner of the room; various spider webs woven from string hung from the ceiling; hundreds of books were stuffed in baskets and on bookshelves; colorful beanbag chairs nearby beckoned readers; an aquarium bubbled quietly in the background; and posters of mentors, such as Martin Luther King, were displayed on the walls. When I stepped into the classroom, the first graders were in the middle of the room practicing a play they had written about Rosa Parks. Chairs were lined in rows to simulate the bus on which Rosa Parks rode that historic day when she refused to give up her seat. Outside, I saw the small garden the children had planted on a once-barren lot in front of the school. The teacher created an environment of wonder and discovery, and the results were tangible as I observed how her students were so engaged and enthusiastic about learning.

We invite you to stand back and observe your classrooms. Where are the places of wonder and discovery? An observation window? A shelf displaying shells, rocks, and other natural objects? Are there living creatures (including plants) that children care for and observe? What places in the classroom would the children mark a wonder *X* on? And if we extend our wonder maps beyond the classroom, are there any natural resources near your classroom that the children could visit and explore?

Our children's lives run the risk of becoming two dimensional in the present day's technology-driven society. The worlds of Internet and video games are becoming just as substantial to children as their reality. One student in San Diego commented that he liked to play indoors because that's where all the electrical outlets are (from Richard Louv's *The Last Child in the Woods*). Classrooms can provide alternative environments to lure young children into continuing their passion for learning. Creating a "wonder" classroom environment is the foundation from which deeper and more sustained explorations can take place.

After I gave a workshop on creating a wonder environment, Ms. Buck, a wonderful primary teacher in Canada, wrote to me about setting up a wonder environment in her kindergarten classroom. She sent this letter to the parents explaining and preparing them for the important work the class was embarking on:

> *Our class is planning to launch an exploration of a new theme — The Wonder World. I am hoping this theme will help my students respond to the natural world with wonderment and awe. We will further extend concepts . . . by gathering data through our senses; we will do sound surveys during outdoor walks; we will look at objects great and small. There will be opportunities for students to wonder, to ask questions, and to pose problems and then we will explore ways to get answers. We will be using our study of the Wonder World as a springboard for math, language, science, art, and music activities.*

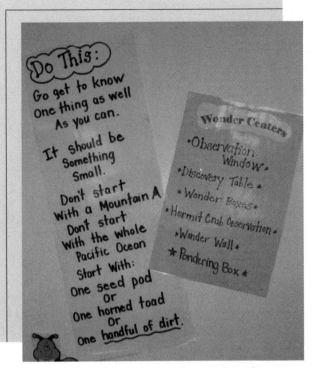

Do This:
Go get to know
One thing as well
As you can.

It should be
Something
Small.

Don't start
With a Mountain
Don't start
With the whole
Pacific Ocean
Start With:
One seed pod
Or
One horned toad
Or
One handful of dirt.

Wonder Centers
•Observation
Window•
•Discovery Table•
•Wonder Boxes•
•Hermit Crab Observation•
•Wonder Wall•
★Pondering Box•

A menu of wonder centers for students to choose from

In this chapter, we map out a menu of ideas to create a "wonder world" that will help encourage children's curiosity and exploration. These ideas can be set up as centers, if you already have the routine of centers established in your classroom, as Jen did; if you don't have center time established, you can introduce these ideas during a nonfiction writing study unit. The questions generated from the centers, as well as the group research on a particular question, model the exploration students will do later on as they write nonfiction. Other teachers have explored wonder centers once a week, and throughout the year, as a way of encouraging curiosity and wonder all year long.

We encourage setting up wonder centers early in the school year so that when any natural wonder occurs—the wind sweeps the leaves off the trees, the snow begins to fall, or a bird lands on the windowsill—the children will be ready to write it down!

Wonder Centers and Projects

1. The Wonder Center

2. Wonder of the Week

3. Pondering Time and Whole-Class Shared Research

4. Pet Observation and Wonder Journals

5. The Discovery Table

6. The Observation Window

7. One Small Square

8. A Listening Walk

9. The Wonder Club

**Curricular and State Standards
Connections to Chapter 1**

✓ Stimulate curiosity

✓ Learn though inquiry

✓ Learn through observation

✓ Gather data through senses

✓ Stimulate imagination and creativity

✓ Respond with wonderment and awe

✓ Find or determine answers to questions derived from curiosity about everyday experiences

✓ Recognize and solve problems through observation and active exploration

---

1. The Wonder Center

I'm more interested in arousing enthusiasm in kids than in teaching the facts. The facts may change, but that enthusiasm for exploring the world will remain with them the rest of their lives.

~ *Seymour Simon*

When my son was younger, he asked many questions whenever we drove in the car together. It was often difficult to drive and concentrate on answering the questions at the same time: "Why is the sky blue?" "Where does rain come from?" "What's in outer space?" As I stopped at intersections or changed lanes on the highway, I tried to explain some of the ways the world

Resource Materials

✓ Large chart

✓ Markers

✓ Sticky notes

worked. I made a promise to myself that I would always do my best to answer each of his questions as thoughtfully as I could. I didn't want to dampen his enthusiasm for exploring the world. Sometimes he would stump me, and I'd have to say, "You know, I don't know the answer; let's look it up when we get home." Some of his questions were deeply spiritual, which surprised me, and made me really think about what I believed.

All young children have an enthusiasm and curiosity about the world that we can nurture at home and in school. We wanted to make a place in the classroom where children could write down their questions during center time or writing workshop time and throughout the day. Questions that are valued by teachers and are then included in the curriculum.

When the kindergartners arrived one morning, Jen had written "The Wonder Center" in big letters on a bulletin board in the back of the room. She placed several yellow sticky note pads and a handful of black pens in a basket on a nearby shelf.

She gathered the children together for morning circle and said, "I've been noticing that you've been asking me so many questions. I'm amazed at all that you wonder about! Your questions keep growing and growing, and so I've decided to set up a center in the classroom where you can write down your questions. I think we'll call it "the wonder center."

The kids turned to one another and smiled. Two boys gave each other high fives.

Jen continued, "The wonder center will be one of our centers during center time. But you can also use the wonder center anytime during the day. When you think of a question, and you want to write it down to remember it for later, you can write it on one of these sticky notes, and then stick it to the wonder center board. Not only that, every Friday we're going to have some time to talk about your questions."

The kids looked at each other wide eyed, with excitement on their faces.

Jen said, "When we have center time today, you can also choose the wonder center as a place to go and jot down the questions you have."

That afternoon during center time three boys, Collin, Kyle, and Ryan, stood at the wonder center and wrote their questions on sticky notes. Collin wrote, "I wonder how slugs are made?" Then Kyle wrote, "How do snakes get their venom?" Ryan connected to Kyle's question and wrote, "How come there are such things as cookie cutter snakes?"

"Oh, I have one," Collin said. "How do snakes shed their skin?"

Ryan said, "I'm on my third or fourth."

"This is awesome!" Kyle said.

After they finished writing, they stuck their questions on the white board. When their ten minutes of center time was up, they moved to the next center, and a new group of students reached for pens and sticky notes on which to write their questions.

One week later, the wonder center board was filled with yellow sticky notes. As we read through their questions, we were amazed at

Varis writes his wonder at the wonder center.

their variety and scope. We decided to revise the center and replace the sticky notes with large chart paper to provide more room for questions. Jen also labeled a gift bag—"the wonder bag"—and placed all the children's sticky note questions into the bag for future discussion.

We encouraged the three boys who were writing about snakes to explore and research their questions. They began their first nonfiction writing piece using questions generated from the wonder center.

Be on the lookout for authentic nonfiction topics that will emerge from the wonder center.

Jen's Reflection

If you don't keep their questions moving through the wonder center, it will get stale and the kids will lose their enthusiasm for asking questions. One of my first-grade colleagues set up a "wonder wall" where she would post the children's questions. The children were given sticky notes to answer one another's questions and then hung their answers next to the question. The kids loved it and looked at it every day to see whose questions were posted and who had answered their question. It was much like the "wonder of the week" discussed in the next section; the difference was that instead of having just one question a week to ponder, the wall features many questions and answers and was changed more frequently.

Kindergartners and first graders might not be able to read many of their own questions; therefore, we asked kids to put their names on every question, so we could go back to them and translate.

2. Wonder of the Week

I have no special talents. I am only passionately curious.

~ *Albert Einstein*

Resource Materials

✓ Large chart with easel

✓ Markers

Friends ate lunch in my back garden as bumblebees buzzed from bee balm to bee balm throughout the afternoon. One of them asked, "Do bumblebees have hearts?" There was silence for a few minutes as we laughed and made up other questions about the bumblebee: "Do bumblebees have lungs?" "Do they have brains?" When our laughter subsided, we pondered what is inside the body of a bumblebee. For days afterward, when we saw one another in town or spoke on the phone, someone would have some new information about bumblebees.

I had a friend in the science department at Cornell University, and I decided to write to him and ask the question, "Does a bumblebee have a heart?" He responded with a long letter, from which I'll paraphrase his answer: Insects have a pump that acts as a primitive heart called a dorsal vessel. It is not involved in moving oxygen around because insects do not have red blood cells. In animals, red blood cells bind with O_2 and transport it where it is needed.

That summer, my friends kept learning more about bumblebees and honeybees.

A few years ago there was a Web site that described itself as "The World Question Center: Fantastically Stimulating—Once You Start You Can't Stop Thinking About That Question!" Thoughtful questions were posted, such as "What are numbers?" and "How is personality made?" People then posted their answers on the site for others to read.

Once when I visited the site I recorded some of the answers that were posted to this question: "What is the most important invention in the last 2000 years?" The answers were unique and varied—the battery, hay, the basket, and languages.

Jen's kindergarten students were writing so many fascinating questions each day at the wonder center that we decided to borrow Edge.org's idea of setting up a wondering community. We designated a center in the classroom where children could think about and respond to a posted question during center time or any free time during the day.

The wonder of the week we posted initially came from one of the children's own questions posted at the wonder center. Children then wrote their explanations on a chart below the question. We later set aside thirty minutes every Friday afternoon for "pondering time" where the class participated in "shared research" and could discuss, research, and write about their ideas on a particular question.

The first wonder of the week came from Ryan, who wrote his question in the wonder center: "How is money made?"

The kindergartners were learning about coins and using money as a counting tool in Everyday Math. We saw the opportunity to connect the wonder center with another area in the curriculum by selecting this question as the wonder of the week.

When we gathered the children on the rug before center time Jen explained how the new center, the wonder of the week, would work. During center time, children could write their theories and thoughts about the highlighted question of the week.

Michael writes his explanation for the wonder of the week: "What kind of animal eats grass?"

"What if we get the answer wrong?" Daisy asked.

"Don't worry," Jen said. "You should just think through your ideas and then we'll discuss it on Friday."

At the start of center time that day, two kids ran to the board and wrote beneath the question, "How Is Money Made?"

Madison wrote, "By a mseny thay squeset/By a machine they squish it."

Ian wrote, "You get a bottle cap and you smushit and you get a magic pen and you draw on it."

By the third day, children were bouncing around so many theories and ideas that discussions commenced throughout the day.

Shayne wrote, "First you get a pes of mettle anthen you smash it soisis flat then you get a speshlie pen and wirethe things thet's is on it." Uma wrote, "It is made by a factory."

Our wonder of the week board was chock full of explanations by week's end, and we gathered the children for pondering time Friday afternoon.

Jen's Reflection

This was one of the easiest centers to create and to keep up with. The children loved coming in each week to find out whose question was being featured and whether they knew anything about the topic. This is a great way to keep questions flowing in your classroom and a great model for how you want the children to approach answers to their questions. The wonder of the week leads into pondering time where I model different ways of finding answers to questions. The use of the wonder of the week and pondering time (to be discussed in the next section) as a whole-class activity is an excellent model to encourage children to explore questions by using some of the research methods to be learned.

3. Pondering Time and Whole-Class Shared Research

My research books come from a fascination with a subject I know only a glimmer about. It can take three years to read, delve, dig, write . . .

~ Aliki

One summer I visited the Museum of Science in Boston and toured an exhibit of Leonardo da Vinci. What really struck me about Leonardo was how curious he was and how many of his inventions had been inspired by his questions. For example, he imagined that someday we could fly like birds, and he posed the question, "How can I make something I can fly in?" He then filled his notebook with sketches of what human flight might look like. He studied how birds and bats flew and then used what he learned to design flying

Resource Materials

✓ Large chart labeled "How We Explore and Answer Questions"

✓ Books about research topic

✓ Internet access to research topic

machines for people. In his notes, he wrote, "Describe underwater swimming and you will have described the flight of birds," according to the museum's exhibit brochure. Leonardo learned from observing the world around him to invent numerous remarkable machines.

We knew that, like Leonardo, it's important to not just ask the questions but to learn to explore questions. We wanted to set up time for the children to ponder their questions and teach them how to go about exploring those questions. We began with a Friday afternoon thinking time as we embarked on modeling the different ways people go about exploring questions.

"Remember when we wrote our wonder of the week on the board and everyone came up with so many answers?" Jen began. "Well, we're going to have time today and every Friday afternoon to discuss some of your thoughts. We can call it Friday afternoon 'thinking time,'" or another word for thinking is 'pondering.'"

The kids seemed excited by this new sophisticated word, "pondering."

"Does anyone remember what you wrote on the board when you were pondering the wonder of the week?"

Pondering = [*L pouderane, weigh*] to think deeply about, consider carefully

Asher stood up. "I wrote, money is made in a factory and shaped in circles," he said.

Jen asked, "How did you know that?"

"I read it in a book."

Jen stopped the class and wrote, "How We Explore Questions" at the top of a chart. Underneath she wrote, "Read or look in a book."

"Did you hear what Asher just said?" Jen asked the class. "'I read it in a book.' That's one way people go about answering and exploring questions. They read and look in books."

Luke raised his hand and said, "You take a piece of metal and you form it in a circle and then you stamp the front and back."

"How do you know that?" Jen asked him.

"I think I saw it on TV once."

Jen wrote, "Watch it on television" on the "How We Explore Questions" chart.

Three hands waved in the air for Jen's attention and a chance to answer her question. She called on Robert.

"I have two answers actually," Robert said. "It comes from mines. It comes from metal."

Jen asked him to explain the word *mines*. "A mine is like a tall, tall mountain," he said. "The rocks on the mountain fall down and get crushed. The rocks go into little pieces the size of a penny, nickel, dime, and quarter. Then they send it to a factory and heat it up and make money. Then they take it into a secret door and . . . it goes into a factory; then they stamp it out, and they shape it, and then they sell it to other people."

Robert then added, anticipating Jen's question, "I saw it in a magazine."

Jen wrote, "Read it in a magazine" on the chart.

Jen thanked Robert for his thoughts and then asked the kids to turn to the person next to them and discuss their thoughts on how money is made. An audible hum filtered through the classroom as they discussed the question.

After a few minutes, Jen called again for the children's attention. She sat in her chair and held up two books. "I went to the library and asked our librarian how I might go about finding an explanation to our question. 'How is money made?' and she gave me two books. This week's wonder, 'How is money made?' is a 'research wonder,' a question that can be answered by thinking but also by looking in books and in magazines or on the computer. So, here I have two books that might be able to help us in discovering the answer."

Jen held up the first book for the class to see. "This one, *The Story of Money*, tells us the history and time line of money."

She read a few sentences from the book and showed several pictures of different kinds of money.

Jen picked up the second book and said, "This one is called *Money*. It tells us that money was first printed in a place called the Bureau of Engraving and Printing. And here is an interesting fact: When paper money gets too old and worn out, they take this old money and burn it."

A few "wows" circulated the room. Jen said, "You see, books are one way to find out the answers to our questions, and these books also gave me new ideas about money. We have two different books, and they each teach us something different about money."

Jen put down the second book and addressed the children again. "I want to talk to you about another way people go about finding explanations to questions and that is by looking up their questions on the Internet."

She then asked everyone to go back to their seats so she could show them something. Jen went to her laptop and turned on the interactive whiteboard. She showed them the U.S. Bureau of Engraving and Printing's Web site. "You're right," she told them. "You kindergartners are so smart! They get the metal for coins from mines. They use fire to melt it, and they use machines to stamp it. There are sixty-five steps in making one dollar. It is a complicated process so people aren't able to do it at home.

"Do you know why dollars are green?" she asked. "It says here that green is used because it doesn't change colors as much as another color might." The Web site showed images of the fronts and backs of a variety of dollars. The kids oohed and ahed.

"We've already learned a lot about how we can find out about our questions," Jen said. "So what have we learned already from our quick research?"

Jen took a fresh piece of chart paper and wrote, "How Is Money Made?"

Robert raised his hand and said, "Coins come from metal from mines."

"They use fire to stamp it," Uma added. "There are sixty-five steps to making dollars."

John waved his hand wildly. "They burn old dollars," he said when Jen called his name.

Jen wrote down everything. "If we were going to write our own book about how money is made, we would do exactly what we just did here in class. We would first think and write down our thoughts like you did during center time. We might also look in books and on the Internet and then gather all the information together and write it down."

She pointed to the chart and said, "Remember, here are some of the ways we can go about researching questions":

How We Explore and Answer Questions

- Read and look in books

- See it on television

- Read and look in magazines

- Look on the bookmarked computer page

"And we used our brains," Uma added.

"That's right," Jen said. "The very first thing you did was think about the question, and you used your brains."

She added "Think" and "Use your brain" to the list.

Jen explained that every Friday we would discuss the wonder of the week. "We'll pull out another question on Monday for us to ponder next week. Eventually, we're going to start writing our own books of wonder."

It was time for dismissal, and the kids gathered their belongings to go home. We had a moment to talk before I gathered my son's things to take home for the weekend. We decided that Friday's pondering time could be an opportunity to teach the children about different types of questions that can be answered by researching in books, computers, television, or observation ("How is money made?") and questions on broader topics ("What makes a best friend?")—which we call heart wonders—that can be answered by using our brains and hearts.

Jen's Reflection

Friday pondering time became a weekly tradition and something the kids looked forward to. They couldn't wait to find out whose question would be asked. To prepare, I took a piece of chart paper and wrote, "How We Explore Research Wonders" and hung it up on the easel at our meeting rug. I chose questions that might integrate our curriculum, questions I knew the kids had a natural curiosity about, and questions we could discuss. We enlisted the help of our school librarians to find books that would help us answer the question and did a quick Google search to see what was on the Internet to share. The Discovery Channel provides a good resource called "Discovery Education Streaming Plus" that has short videos on everything you could imagine for grades K–12. (There is a subscription fee, but it is well worth it.) After sharing and discussing the question with the materials at hand, I encouraged the children to try to investigate the question on their own. I put the question up on the easel and invited the children to bring in any resources they could find to help us answer the question. We left the questions and resources up on the ledge of the easel for the kids to add to and explore until we brought out the next Friday question.

Once the children became comfortable with the process, I moved into having a pondering time most days during our morning meeting. We would pick one of their questions from the bag or the chart and ponder it. Three to five minutes were devoted to thinking, and then kids shared their ideas and answers. It was important for them to know that every question didn't have to be researched and explored through outside sources and that they could teach one another with their beginning knowledge of the world and how they perceived things. It was also an interesting way to get to know the kids, their life experiences, and their beliefs. Some questions led to interesting conversations. I watched as my students' curiosity grew, how they began to listen to each other because they were interested in an answer, and how their answers would build off of one another. We would have this daily pondering time for a month or so, take a break, and then go back to it to keep it fresh and new. I found that the kids would miss the time and would ask for it on our months off.

4. Pet Observation and Wonder Journals

She observed how [her pet rabbits] rested, how they nested or hibernated, and the characteristics of their play.

~ Linda J. Lear (on Beatrix Potter)

Near our house is a turtle hospital where loggerhead, leatherback, and green turtles are rescued from the sea and brought to recuperate. Until I visited the marine life center, I didn't know how often turtles need to be rescued. Some turtles get caught in fishing line; some get cut by boat propellers; some simply stop eating. Whenever friends and family with children visit us, we take them to the turtle hospital and lean over into the big turtle tanks to see how our favorite turtles are doing. All children fall in love with the turtles and love watching them swim around the tanks. Shimano, one of our favorites, was named after the fishing rod he dragged for miles.

Resource Materials

✓ Pets: caterpillars, fish, ant farms, guinea pig
✓ Journals that lie flat
✓ Thin markers

Jen, as many primary teachers do, acquired several pets in her classroom. We found that displaying journals near the class pets around the room became an outlet for children to write down their observations and to share their ideas and questions about these living creatures. The journals also helped sharpen observation skills. We read from these observation journals periodically and discussed thoughts or questions the children may have had during morning meeting. Three of these journals are described next.

Snowy

The first journal centered on Snowy, the class guinea pig. The kindergarten children in Jen's class gathered around Snowy every free moment and noticed every move she made: "She's sleeping." "Her nose is wiggling." "She's buried herself under the chips." We listened to the children talk and discovered there was a class full of scientists and writers using details. The students observed their guinea pig with keen eyes every day and discussed their questions and observations out loud. We wanted to encourage them to write down their observations and thoughts. "Snowy's Adventures" began as a journal for children to keep a daily record of observations and questions about Snowy and any questions they had about her. This activity also became a choice for center time.

Figure 1.1

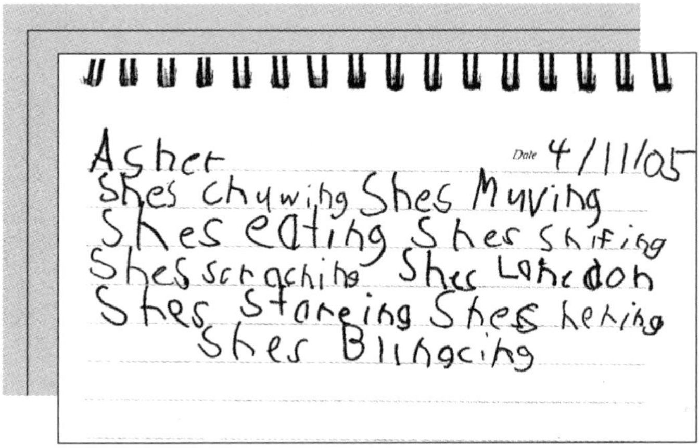

Asher's journal page about Snowy: "She's chewing. She's moving. She's eating. She's sniffing. She's scratching. She's lonesome. She's staring. She's hearing. She's blinking."

In one month, they had written a wonderful account of their guinea pig, complete with vignettes, observations, and examples of poetic and descriptive writing. Periodically, Jen read the entries from this class journal out loud to the children and discussed some of their observations and questions (see Figure 1.1).

Wendy

The second observation journal focused on Wendy, the small Chinese fighting fish who arrived one morning in a small fishbowl. Jordon had received Wendy as a party favor from a birthday celebration but wasn't able to keep the fish at home. The class's newest observation journal, "Wendy's Adventures," was born. Although Wendy was small, and she lived in such a small environment (a fishbowl), she inspired a multitude of stories, observations, and questions. For example, one day Jen and the class took Wendy out to the playground for her very own recess, but the fire alarm rang and Wendy was evacuated with the rest of the class. In the chaos of trying to find their emergency location, someone accidentally knocked Wendy's bowl over, and she spilled out onto the grass. Amid the screams and panic of five- and six-year-olds, the children quickly rescued her and scooped her up with a name tag. After that incident, Wendy's life inside her fishbowl was safe and secure on the shelf near the window.

The Caterpillar Mystery Book

One Tuesday morning in January, the usually reserved and thoughtful Madison came bursting into the room. She had a huge smile on her face as she handed an envelope to Jen.

"My mom wrote you a note," Madison said.

Jen opened the envelope and read the note from Madison's mom. Madison had received a butterfly kit as a Christmas gift and wanted to bring it in to school so the whole class could be a part of the experience. She wrote back right away asking Madison's mom to please send it in. The class would be thrilled. Madison beamed and ran off to tell her friends, Shayne and Annie, of the great event that would be unfolding.

The next day Madison brought in the butterfly kit along with another note explaining that the caterpillars had been ordered and would be here in three to four weeks. Finally, after weeks of waiting, the caterpillars arrived. The kids were all abuzz that morning as they read the sign on the classroom door: "The caterpillars have arrived in Mrs. McDonough's class."

Questions started immediately. "Why are they so small?" "How many eyes do they have?" "Are those webs in there, like a spider's?"

As Jen gathered the children close on the rug, she told them how exciting this caterpillar adventure was going to be and that she had noticed those asking questions and sharing ideas about what would be happening. She showed them a booklet (ten white pieces of typing paper, folded and stapled) and said, "I think you all need to write down your questions and anything you observe, so we never forget all of our great thinking."

She asked the kids what the book should be called and Leo came up with the "Caterpillar Mystery Book." We all thought this was a good name because we just weren't sure what was going to happen with these caterpillars. It was a mystery to us all.

Jen first modeled how to write questions and observations in the "Caterpillar Mystery Book." She turned to the first page of the booklet. "When you come to the book to write down your thoughts, the first thing you need to do is write your name so that we can go back and talk to you about it later. Another great thing to do is to write the date so we know exactly when you were looking at the caterpillars."

Then she turned to look at the caterpillars and said, "Okay, now I am going to look very carefully at this cup of caterpillars and draw exactly what I see." Of course, a chorus of voices chimed in.

"Don't forget to draw the green stuff at the bottom."

"Make sure you draw all five of the caterpillars."

After a few moments of frantic sketching to get all the details, Jen turned back to the class. "All right, I drew what I saw. Now I need to think about any questions I have or things I see. Hmm. I am really wondering what the web is for. I am going to write that down.

"Who else is wondering something?" Jen called on Blake, whose hand was waving wildly in the air.

"Can you write this down?" Blake asked. "I wonder where the caterpillar's eyes are."

Jen logged Blake's question in the "Caterpillar Mystery Book." After a few more questions and observations, Jen closed the book and placed it next to the butterfly house. She told the children that right before school, during center time, and right after school were perfect times to record their thoughts in the "Caterpillar Mystery Book" (see Figure 1.2).

Pages were filling up by week's end, and Jen read the kids' recordings. Many were well thought out, such as Shawn's. On January 27, he guessed that maybe the caterpillars use the webs to make a cocoon. On January 30, Shayne wrote, "I wonder when they are going to make their cocoons" (see Figure 1.3).

Figure 1.2

Title page of the "Caterpillar Mystery Book"

Figure 1.3

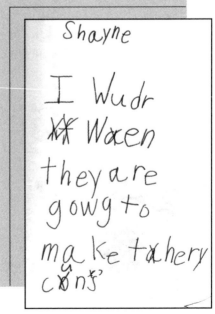

Shayne's page from the "Caterpillar Mystery Book"

And when the caterpillars made their cocoons, Luke recorded it in the book (see Figure 1.4).

Once or twice a week during morning meeting Jen would look through the "Caterpillar Mystery Book" to discuss what was going on and to try to answer the kids' questions. "I noticed that a lot of you are writing down your thinking in our 'Caterpillar Mystery Book.'" Jen told them, "A lot of us are wondering about the webs in the cup and why the caterpillars make them." She pulled out the booklet that came with the butterfly kit. "It says here that caterpillars spin webs to help them move around inside the cup. What a smart idea. Does anyone have any other ideas about why the caterpillars spin webs?"

"Maybe they use the web to make their cocoon," Shayne said. "Like spiders use webs to wrap up insects they're going to eat."

Jen asked her how she came up with that idea. "Oh, that's easy. I read about it in my spider book," she said.

Figure 1.4

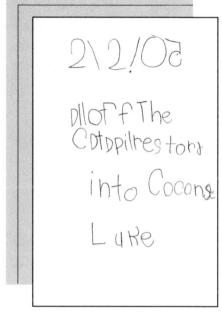

Luke's page from the "Caterpillar Mystery Book": "A lot of the caterpillars turn into cocoons."

"What a great idea, Shayne. You thought about what you already knew and used it to think about the caterpillars."

Jen sent the kids off with the idea that everyone should be looking through the caterpillar and butterfly books to answer some of the questions. They would talk about it during the next morning meeting.

As the caterpillars grew and changed, the observation book did too. On February 2, Luke recorded that all the caterpillars were now in cocoons, and on February 9, Ian wrote, "Two of the butterflies are out, and a flower is in the house for them to eat." The last entry was on February 10. On that day, we took the butterflies outside to the butterfly garden and said goodbye. As we watched the butterflies fly away, I thought about the transformation they had undergone in just a few weeks. I also thought about the kids. Through this one activity, they had become careful observers and determined answer seekers.

Jen's Reflection

Many of us have had wonderful and sometimes exotic pets in our classrooms for these reasons: to inspire responsibility, camaraderie, and wonder in our kids. The journals were a simple and easy way to inspire kids to write down their thinking and questions about the pets they saw every day and to help them see with new eyes. The journals became a place to record discoveries and to explore new questions.

5. The Discovery Table

I think the journal itself has taught me to revere the ordinary.

~ *Hannah Hinchman*

Resource Materials

✓ *The Other Way to Listen* by  Byrd Baylor

✓ Small table or shelf

✓ Letter to go home (*Appendix*)

✓ Magnifying glass

✓ Nature objects: acorns, shells, flowers, etc.

✓ Discovery sheets (*Appendix*)

In Rachel Carson's book *The Sense of Wonder* (1965), she explores the natural world of Maine with her three-year-old grandnephew. She writes, "And then there is the world of little things, seen all too seldom. Many children, perhaps because they themselves are small and lower to the ground then we, notice and delight in the small and inconspicuous. . . . An investment of a few dollars in a good hand lens or magnifying glass will bring a new world into being. With your child, look at objects you take for granted as commonplace or uninteresting. A sprinkling of sand grains may appear as gleaming jewels" (76).

I first explored the discovery table center in a New York City classroom with Rachel Carson's sense of wonder in mind. Children in the school were eager to observe and to experience the natural world. I brought a bag of shells into a second-grade classroom and watched as a small circle of students formed around the shells. The kids who were closest to the shells touched their shiny surfaces and placed the shells next to their ears to hear ocean sounds. I heard kids oohing and ahing in wonder. During center time, kids took a few shells from the discovery table and lay on the floor on their stomachs with notebooks and a pen to record their observations. This was their favorite center. It was a chance to linger with treasures from the natural world so vastly different from the congested streets below their second-grade classroom windows.

We wanted to create a discovery center in Jen's kindergarten class, so we sent home a letter to the parents of her class, asking the kids to bring in their own beloved objects from nature:

A discovery table in a kindergarten classroom

Dear Wonderers,

We will be turning our classroom into a place of wonder. A place to: observe, ask questions, and study the natural world. This is one way we become inspired to write! Please bring in a beloved object of nature — an acorn, a shell, a nest, a bone, a shark's tooth, a piece of pine, a flower — that you've chosen because you think it is beautiful, it makes you wonder, or it amazes you. We will use these items to create a discovery center where we will observe, question, and appreciate one another's natural treasures. Take your time to choose something really special to you and bring it in to share! We look forward to finding out what inspires you!

It didn't take long. Treasures began arriving the next morning. Ryan proudly showed his starfish to Kyle, who in turn held up his coconut and announced, "It's from the tree in my front yard." One by one, the treasures arrived that week: shells brought back from vacations at the beach, a vibrant peacock feather, a sea biscuit, and a set of teeth purportedly from dinosaurs that lived in Australia. The kids placed each precious item on the discovery table, and discussions charged with excitement commenced immediately.

The students brought in many different items that were of interest to them to hang by the discovery table: an X-ray of one student's broken arm, Giovanni's gecko poster, and a copy of a Time *magazine article from the early 1900s that featured one of Jen's student's great-great-grandfathers.*

Jen tried to find nonfiction books to place at the discovery table that went along with the items brought in so the children could learn more about their objects.

The discovery table changed from year to year. Sometimes it was a table in the middle of the room, but this year the discovery table was a shelf above the children's cubbies in front of the window. The children covered it with painted self-portraits and poetry they wrote about the objects and an observation journal to keep observations and questions.

The discovery table grew with each recess as pockets were emptied and new treasures were placed on the shelf. Shawn found a beetle for the class to study; Kyle found an oddly shaped piece of plastic; and Kelly and Annie always made sure the class had fresh field flowers (weeds) available for closer inspection.

The children frequently gathered around the discovery table to view the treasures. A magnifying glass and journal were placed on the table, and Jen asked children to look closely and record their observations and discoveries.

As Jen listened to the children's conversations during center time, their words were filled with detailed language. Robert said about a sea biscuit, "There are little tiny shells inside that can fit through the hole in the center. Look, the small dots at the top make the shape of a horse!"

The other children around him had a lot of questions for Robert: "How big does it get?" "Is there an animal in there?" "How does a sea biscuit grow in the ocean?"

Jen read an excerpt from Byrd Baylor's *The Other Way to Listen* (1997) in which a young boy listens to the advice of an elderly man meant to inspire the children to observe the objects carefully:

> *Do this*
> *go get to know*
> *one thing*
> *as well*
> *as you can.*
> *It should be something small.*
> *Don't start*
> *with a mountain*
> *don't start*
> *with the whole Pacific Ocean.*
> *Start with*
> *one seed pod*
> *or*
> *one dry weed*
> *or*
> *one horned toad*
> *or one handful*
> *of dirt. (15)*

Figure 1.5

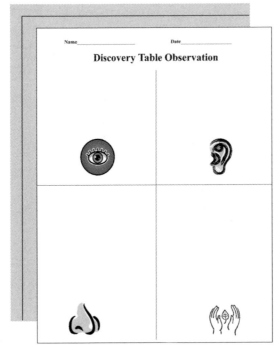

Discovery Table Observation sheet

Figure 1.6

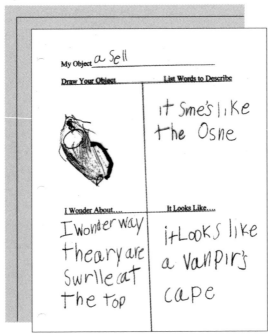

The second version of the discovery sheet asks students to look closely at their objects and respond in four different ways.

We posted two different kinds of discovery observation sheets to encourage the children to get to know their objects as well as they could and to record these observations. The first observation sheet asked children to record their sensory observations: smell, sight, touch, and hearing (see Figure 1.5; also in Appendix).

The second discovery observation sheet asked children to study and look closely at their objects in four different ways (a blank version can be found in the Appendix). The first box asks children to draw their object, not to make a perfect drawing but to linger and look even more closely and to discover details that they might have missed at first glance. The second box asks children to list words that describe their object. The third box asks children to write down any wonders or questions they have. And the fourth box asks children to make analogies or similes about what their objects look like (see Figure 1.6).

The discovery center was the most sought-after center during center time, and the children's writing was detailed and often poetic as well.

Jen's Reflection

The discovery center was a huge success with the children. I made sure to have them discuss each of their pieces with their friends so they would all understand the significance and uniqueness of each object. I treated each child's donation as a "treasure" so that they would treat one another's objects with respect and care.

It's important to model the discovery sheet a few times so the children understand what you are asking them to do; otherwise, they won't go into a lot of detail with the object they are observing. We took one writing workshop time to have the class fill out individual discovery sheets about their own objects, making sure to model with the whole group first. I conferred with them as they were looking closely at their objects and writing what they saw. In my conference, I would try to draw out the aspects of their objects that weren't necessarily the first things they saw. I would ask, "What else do you see?" "Look closely. What does that part remind you of?"

Placing small magnifying glasses at the center encouraged the kids to look deeply at the object instead of focusing on the superficial. Instead of writing "My shell is hard and white," a child using a magnifying glass is more likely to write, "My shell has tiny holes, circle bumps, and has bits of dirt or sand stuck to it."

A small table or top of a shelf is all that is needed for the discovery table. They kept the items there for about a month before I would encourage everyone to switch their objects out. Most of the kids would do this on their own as they found things after school or on the weekends that they wanted to add. Some items of great interest stayed all year, such as the beehive that had come off of Alex's house, the rock collection one of the teachers had brought in, and the seahorse that Katie and Jack's mom found on the beach.

Connect books to their objects. When Harry brought in his collection of miniature stones, we found a book on rocks and minerals, and he read the book to see whether he could find his stones. This connection prepared the class for nonfiction writing. They see that books have been written about objects that they are passionate about.

6. The Observation Window

The real voyage of discovery consists not in seeking new landscapes, but in having new eyes.

~ *Marcel Proust*

Resource Materials

✓ Classroom or hallway window

✓ Crepe paper for window outlining

✓ Journals that open flat

✓ Thin markers

When I lived in New York City, the bay window in my living room looked out at a maple tree. I watched its leaves change from bright orange and fuchsia in the fall to bare winter gray. Every spring, even with snow still falling, I would watch for the first green buds to appear and knew that spring wasn't far off. Living with the maple tree outside my window helped me connect to the natural world in the city. It was my lifeline to the changing seasons and to the natural beauty of New York.

When I worked in schools in New York City, many of the classrooms set up observation windows where children could observe and then write about those observations.

Harry and Caroline at the observation window in Jen's classroom

Creating an observation window gives children the opportunity to look at their world outside the classroom window and to write about what they see, hear, and wonder about. Perhaps your view outside the classroom is apartment buildings, a city skyline, a maple tree, or a parking lot, but whatever it is, children can record their observations and questions about the world outside the classroom.

We set up the observation window center by outlining part of Jen's classroom window with crepe paper. We placed an observation and wonder journal on the shelf next to the window with a cup of pencils and markers nearby. We invited children to write and draw what they saw and heard and to write their wonders about the world outside the classroom.

We watched as a group of three children stood at the observation window during center time and talked about what they observed. It was a windy day, and the kids noticed how the wind blew the trees. Shawn looked up toward the sky as he watched clouds moving quickly across, and he picked up a pen and wrote in the observation journal, "I wonder how the sky moves?" Asher drew the wind in wavy lines and then wrote on the side of the page, "How does the wind blow?" (see Figure 1.7).

The observation window was a popular center choice, and the observation journal began to fill up quickly. The children drew what they saw and asked questions that would be discussed during Friday pondering time.

Figure 1.7

Asher's page from the observation window journal

Jen's Reflection

This center was the easiest to get started and stayed new and exciting because what children notice in the outside world constantly changes.

Other ways to keep the window inviting are to

- Hang a bird feeder to attract different kinds of birds to the window
- Plant flowers that attract butterflies
- Hang poems about the outside world and quotes from the observation journal around the window
- Frame the observation window to make it a special place in the classroom

I encourage several kids to be at the observation window at the same time, as the conversations inspire them to write more in their journals. Sometimes the kids work together on one page, or each child takes a side in the notebook and writes his or her own observations at the same time. I also keep markers by the window for the children to sketch what they see outdoors.

7. One Small Square

Amazing things are all around me, appearing ordinary at first, until I really look at them closely.

~ *Joanne Ryder*

Resource Materials

✓ *One Small Square* by Donald Silver

✓ Cardboard cutout squares

✓ Small 3-by-5-inch spiral flip-top notebooks

✓ Sharp pencils

✓ Basket by door to keep notebooks

One evening as we were walking our dog on the beach, my son suddenly stopped and yelled, "Look!" We froze in our tracks and saw leatherback hatchling turtles crawling out of their underground nest. The nest was near a pile of seaweed, and I might have walked right past them if it hadn't been for my son's voice. As Rachel Carson observed, children are lower to the ground so they often notice things that adults don't.

We knelt down beside the nest to watch the little hatchlings crawl out and scramble over seaweed and small mounds toward the roiling ocean waves. We watched until all the hatchlings were swallowed up and safely swimming away from shore.

Jen and I discussed how we wanted the kids to begin noticing what's right under their feet. Jen gave a mini-lesson to introduce a new idea that would help them become more aware of what was around them. "Sometimes we forget to see things around us. Most people don't even think of looking closely at what's around us. They might just see grass or dirt or ocean sand, but if they were to look closely, who knows what they might find."

For the mini-lesson, Jen introduced the book *One Small Square: Backyard* (1993), which is part of the One Small Square nonfiction series by Donald M. Silver. The book points out how there's more to be seen if you look closely at the world around you. The author describes one small square in a backyard, a forest, a seashore, and so on, and invites children to smell, to listen, and to look at the world around them closely. Although the books are written for children seven years old and up, Jen reads them parts of the book to describe the process:

> *Go outside and catch a dandelion seed zigzagging to the ground. Pick up a rock that crumbles in your fingers. Look for tracks left in mud by an ovenbird. Listen to a cricket rub its wings together.*

> *Explore just one small square of a backyard—your own or someone else's—and you will uncover clue after clue about how nature works. (1993, 3–5)*

Jen held up a square we cut. "Today, you each are going to get a square like the square on the front of *One Small Square*. Your job will be to lay the square down outside and observe really closely what you can see in your square. Remember you are looking very closely. Once you have really looked, you can start writing down what you see in this small field notebook."

Jen held out a small bound notebook. John wanted to know whether they could keep their field notebooks and take them home. We told them that eventually they could, but first they were going to learn how to use them.

I showed them a page of my own field notebook and what I had observed outside the classroom (see Figure 1.8).

Figure 1.8

5/13

I saw grass.
Over 20 blades.

Underneath is the
dirt.
Do they have roots?
How does grass grow?
What's underneath?

The dirt is black. It
smells moist.

I saw a tiny spider
crawling in the grass.
What kind of spider
is it?

A page from Georgia's notebook that models looking at one small square of grass

One small square on the grass

Donald Silver gives more instruction, which we read to the children:

> *Sit in your square and close your eyes. What sounds can you hear? What do you smell? Sounds and smells are important clues to which birds are visiting, if the wind is blowing, or if the soil is damp. Write them down. (1993, 9)*

After some careful modeling on the classroom rug the children grabbed a square, a notebook of their own, and a pencil. They lined up to go outside, and we reminded them, "Good observers don't just look with their eyes. They use their ears, their hands, all of their senses."

Once outside, the kids fanned out in every direction. Some dashed to their favorite place, like Annie who headed straight to the fishpond, and Daisy who loved the shadow of the big banyan tree. Others found new places to explore. Each child settled quickly in a spot, eager to begin.

As we walked around, we took time to watch the kids as they observed. We noticed that some kids described effortlessly every item they saw in their one small square. They were already using colors, sizes, and textures in their descriptions. We made a note to put these kids in a strategy lesson later to make sure they were transferring this skill to their writing. While these kids kept working, there were others who simply sat and stared. John especially seemed strained by this activity. Jen approached him and asked how it was going. He told her that all he could see was grass, and the concern was evident by his facial expression. He wanted to know, "Should there be more to this?"

Kindergartners observe grass through one small square.

It was important to let John know that he was perfectly on track in his observations; that the first way we learn to observe is to see the big picture. "John, how smart of you to notice all the great grass in your square." Jen told him, and he sat up a little straighter. She decided he was ready to be guided a little further and asked him to think a bit. "Remember when we were getting ready to come outside and Ms. Heard reminded us that careful observers don't just use their eyes, but they also use their noses, ears, and hands?"

"Oh, I can touch it and describe how the grass feels," he said. Immediately, his hand reached out to the closest blade of grass. "It feels smooth and a little sharp on this part."

Jen encouraged him to write down everything that he felt, and then she moved to confer with another child. There are ways we can encourage students if they don't come up with any observations on their own. We showed them how to look even more closely and modeled what we saw. We were hopeful that this project would illustrate how children can write with more details. We often reminded the children of the details they saw and wrote about from this project.

After ten minutes, we gathered the kids back inside on the rug to discuss what they noticed. Again, we took careful notes on who wrote down details and who still used broad terms in their descriptions.

We were amazed at the children's detailed observations.

We decided that while others might have seen just grass, we saw:

- A worm that is brown and white

- Two ants

- A crystal

- A leaf shaped like a swan

- A rock with words on it

- A yellow bug

- A dead fly

- A white root that was really squiggly like stairs going up and down

- Soil

- A rock like a moon rock

- Veins on a leaf

Our goal was that the kids' newfound skills in looking for details would carry over into their writing pieces and later into their poetry. We had recently been talking to the kids about adding details to their writing, and it occurred to us that maybe we were asking them to do something they didn't yet know. If their observations of the world around them—and recordings of their observations—were general and vague, how could we expect details in their writing pieces during writing workshop? We realized that explicitly showing kids how to get up close and focus in on one thing would lead to writing with more detail.

The field notebooks and squares went in a special basket right by the door so the kids could easily grab them on the way out to recess for more observation. We reminded them that they should use their new skills and always observe the world around them—not just the big stuff, but the littlest of things as well. The field notebooks and small squares became a favorite recess activity for many of them.

Note: You can do this project in urban schools as well. I first introduced using one small square as an observation tool in New York City. One of the teachers I worked with took her students to Central Park to initiate this project. After their initial excitement about being outside, the children settled down and began to observe. Other places in the city that would work are sidewalks and grassy patches in the schoolyard.

Jen's Reflection

The field journals were tiny spiral-bound notebooks, and the "squares" were black pieces of construction paper cut to look like a frame. I asked the kids to put their squares with their field journals (folded and tucked inside) so they had them when they went to observe.

Getting emergent writers to independently begin to include more detail in their writing is something that my colleagues and I have discussed as a goal over the years of teaching writing. We reference the one small square project during conferring to encourage kids to write with more detail. For example, "Remember when at first all you saw was a piece of grass but then when you looked a little more you saw things like white roots and lines in the green stalks? Well, it's the same thing with your piece about going on a roller coaster at the fair. Right now, you have just told your reader that you went to a roller coaster and that's it. Help them to see more, like how it twists and turns, how fast it went, exactly what you just told me. Help your reader see more than just the roller coaster by including more details."

---

8. A Listening Walk

*I believe children can be helped to hear many voices about them.
Take time to listen and talk about the voices of the earth and what they mean —
the majestic voice of thunder, the winds, the sound of surf or flowing streams.*

~ *Rachel Carson*

> **Resource Materials**
>
> ✓ *The Listening Walk* by Paul Showers
>
> ✓ Clipboards
>
> ✓ Paper
>
> ✓ Pens or pencils

I sneaked into Jen's class one morning armed with one of my favorite books, *The Listening Walk* by Paul Showers (1993). Jen and I were taking the kids on a listening walk. We would pay careful attention to our surroundings with our ears and then write from our observations once we returned to the classroom.

We settled the children on the rug, and I pulled them in closer. Using my softest voice, I told them that one thing writers do is listen so carefully that they hear what no one else can hear. Then they can say it in a way that no one has ever said it before. Our listening walk would help us sharpen our ears.

"It's like when you wrote 'Frog Serenade,'" Robert jumped in. "Instead of saying, 'ribbit, ribbit,' you said 'ga-lunk, ga-lunk.' You said it in a different way."

"That's right, Robert. Very smart." I laughed and kept going. "Today I am going to share with you *The Listening Walk* by Paul Showers." *The Listening Walk* was a perfect book to demonstrate what I hoped the children would do. In this book, a little girl takes a walk with her father, but instead of looking and seeing with her eyes, she pays attention to what she hears with her ears. "Listen to what she hears," I told them. "Because after we read the book we're going on our own listening walk."

I read the story as the kids quieted down and tried to sharpen their ears as suggested. Of course, they couldn't help but join in to make lawn mower and sprinkler noises. Leo chimed in with his affection for the author's use of unusual words to describe sounds like "twick," "dop," and "zzzzzs" and "oooos."

"Can you imagine that the girl in the book is such a great listener that she could hear the difference between two different kinds of sprinklers or types of cars?" I asked the class. They nodded their heads, and I kept reading.

When I finished, I asked the kids to be very quiet and listen for everything they could hear in the classroom. Ian heard the air conditioner. Ryan heard the guinea pig drinking. Uma heard the tapping of a pencil.

"You could say it like a poet, Uma," I suggested. "Tapping like a woodpecker on a tree." Uma nodded in agreement.

Finally, we lined up for our listening walk, the children armed with clipboards, paper, and pencils. We are lucky; outside the classroom is a courtyard with three big banyan trees, a fishpond complete with koi fish, and a butterfly garden. The children quickly dispersed to different corners of the courtyard and got busy listening. Luke headed straight for the banyan tree and climbed into a little nook surrounded by strangler figs and leaves. Annie, John, and Shawn headed to the fishpond to "sharpen their ears" and listen for inspiration.

Georgia observes young writers during the listening walk.

I had already told the children that they would be writing a class poem about their listening walk once we were back in the classroom. But as Jen and I walked around, we realized that the children had already begun writing poems on their own.

Below are a few students' poems inspired by the fishpond.

Sssssssssss. . . .
The fish was talking to me.
Bloop, bloop, bloop.
Talk bubbles.
The fish said Hi!

~ Shawn

I hear
a
fish
glistening
in a pond
with
fish
and
ducks

~ *Annie*

And Bella's listening poem about the wind:

Wind Shhh
Shhhh
Wind like an ice cube
Shhhh
Wind strong
Shhhh
Wind like a storm
Shhhh
Wind cool

We let the children write for about fifteen minutes outside and then asked them to gather their clipboards and meet us back inside on the rug.

Once inside, I let them know how impressed I was. "Wow, writers! I thought we would be writing a piece together, but you guys did your own writing. You are amazing."

The kids took turns reading their writing aloud, and Jen and I would look at each other in amazement. They not only sharpened their ears, but they also sharpened their observational, writing, and poetry skills.

I asked the kids whether we should take another listening walk, and everyone put their thumbs up. "What other kinds of walks could we go on?" I asked them.

"A seeing walk."

"A touching walk."

Clearly, the listening walk had inspired these kindergarten writers.

Note: You don't have to have a banyan tree and butterfly garden outside to go for a listening walk. City sidewalks and even open city windows reveal a variety of sounds: cars honking, buses roaring, people walking, jackhammers banging, and voices shouting.

Jen's Reflection

One thing we encouraged the children to do on this particular walk was to close their eyes. It seemed to help heighten their sense of hearing.

Very young writers can draw instead of write or make a list of what they hear. Their observations can then be transformed into shared writing when you return to the classroom. Save the writing from year to year so children can notice what other classes found on their walks and pay attention to how things were similar or different from what they saw or heard.

These kinds of walks, where the children focus on just using one of their senses, helped my kids start to hone their sense of details in writing. Each child through drawing or writing was able to capture what they noticed and admired.

9. The Wonder Club

Over three hundred years ago, the poet Matsuo Basho said, "To learn about a tree, go to a tree." Basho was considering more than the scientific facts you learn about trees. He was suggesting that the creatures of the natural world speak a language, one perhaps different from yours, but one you can understand if you listen with your imagination.

～ Lorraine Ferra

"I'm going to start my own wonder club," Jamie told Jen and me one day. "A wonder club where we talk about all of our wonders."

Jamie thought of this idea all on her own, and Jen encouraged her to follow through and make a sign-up sheet for the class.

Jamie was building up excitement at lunch that day as she stood in line holding her lunch box. She whispered to the kids about her great idea, and they responded with enthusiasm and promises of "I'll be in your club." Jen and I had high hopes that Jamie's wonder club would be a hit. Because of Jamie, the energy and enthusiasm produced by creating and exploring wonders were bouncing their way out the door with the kids.

As the kids came in from lunch, we watched as Andres and Margo ran over to Jamie's newly minted sign-up sheet and added their names. This brought the grand total of the wonder club membership up to three.

The next day, during center time, the three wonderers met on the reading rug. The wonder conversation began as the rest of the kids were involved in the other centers. This was the perfect time for Jen and me to sneak in and listen to the first meeting of the wonder club.

"I'm going to ask you a question first," Jamie told Andres and Margo. She had prepared by gathering some of the wonders she had placed at the wonder center. "Why does my mom make me cut my hair so short?"

Margo was the first to bite. "I think it's because she wants you to have nice hair."

"Maybe there isn't enough blood getting to your hair, so your hair doesn't grow," Andres added.

"Blood doesn't go out of your head like that," Jamie objected, but she was quickly diverted as she read another wonder, "Why do we have to go to school?"

"We need to learn," said Margo.

"So we don't get arrested," Andres finished. "But what about homeschool?"

Before anyone could answer, Margo informed the others that it was her turn to ask the questions. She looked through her sticky notes and asked, "How does God make teeth?"

Jamie and Andres thought about this one for a second.

"They just grow into your mouth," said one.

"It happens when you chew," said another.

Margo grabbed the class copy of *No, David* by David Shannon off the ledge behind her and flipped to the page showing David's pointy teeth. "Do these teeth look normal to you?" she asked.

The three members of the wonder club exploded in hushed giggles as Jen and I excused ourselves to check on other centers. As I made my way around the room, I heard them arguing over the best answer to why we need clothes. These wonderers were asking some questions that I'd never thought to ask, but I loved the thinking that went into their answers.

A wonder club can include discussions of questions and reading books to explore questions, followed by the group writing their thoughts down in a book or on a large chart to display in the room.

This was only the beginning. The children were focused, energized, and excited about sharing their ideas with one another. My hope was that they would take this experience, share it with others, and learn how to grow ideas through conversations throughout the school day in all subject matters. Our goal was to include the wonder club as of one of the after-school clubs in the school.

Jen's Reflection

I was thrilled when Jamie came up with the wonder club idea. It demonstrated that she was paying attention to the kind of work we were exposing them to and that she understood the fun and wonderment of asking and answering questions. Up to this point in the year, we had been having informal book clubs once a week in which the kids were able to create sign-up sheets based on certain topics, authors, or series books they might meet about and discuss with fellow readers. Jamie impressed me with her ability to integrate the wonder center ideas into an original idea for a club.

Introducing Wonder Ideas

When:

✓ Wonder centers can be integrated into centers you already have in place.

OR

✓ Wonder centers can be introduced as a whole-class activity during writing workshop time.

OR

✓ Wonder Centers can be set up in the morning for children as they arrive.

✓ Introduce wonder centers early in the school year so there will be places for kids to write down their wonders.

How:

✓ Introduce one center a day as a whole-class activity.

✓ Create a list of wonder centers and add to the list as you introduce new centers.

✓ Place index cards with four or five children's names on each card for each center in a pocket chart.

✓ Guide children when they arrive in the morning to go to the center displaying their name.

✓ Move the cards each day so children will finish all five wonder centers by the end of the week.

✓ Allow children to work in centers for between five and ten minutes.

✓ Repeat instructions of what kind of activities they should be doing at each center.

After the first week, children know the routines enough to be in centers independently. Collect whatever work was generated at the centers or take some time to look through the observation journals to see what the kids were writing about.

Children's Talk: Inquiry Conversations

Unlike the picture of hushed children that I portray in my poem "Straight Lines," we use recommendations from the American Association for the Advancement of Science (AAAS) to encourage young children to talk with one another during center time, to participate enthusiastically in whole-group discussions, and to discuss their wonder explorations during independent work time.

An article published by the AAAS states, "In the early grades, children's conversations and discussions constitute perhaps the single richest source of evidence to teachers concerning the substance of their students' ideas . . . It's the many little conversations among children that really count . . . in promoting their ideas and observations" (Chittenden and Jones 1999).

Here are guidelines for facilitating discussions:

1. Discussions (either small-group, whole-group, or one-on-one conferences) begin with open-ended questions:

    - What have you noticed lately about Snowy the guinea pig?

    - What did you discover today?

    - What were your wonders today?

    - What was your thinking about your wonders?

2. Let children guide the discussion.

    Allowing children to follow the thread of their own and one another's ideas and thinking will help deepen the discussion and allow you a window into their understandings. Jen and I frequently asked questions during conferences and discussions:

    - How do you know that?

    - What makes you think that?

    - What do you think of what _____ said?

    - Do you think that's true? Why?

3. Encourage all children to participate in small- and whole-group discussions.

As we sat in a circle on the rug for a whole-group discussion, we asked children to go around the circle so that every child had a chance to participate. If a child was silent for most of the discussion, we would ask respectfully:

- What's your thinking on this?
- What do you think about _____'s idea?

4. Record children's talk.

Jen and I took copious notes when children were talking with each other. This helped us understand their thinking and helped us remind them of what they knew about a topic when they wrote nonfiction pieces.

Books for Creating a Wonder World

Aliki. 1989. *My Five Senses*. Let's-Read-And-Find-Out Science series, Stage 1. New York: HarperCollins.

Allen, Judy. 2002. *Are You an Ant*? Backyard Book series. New York: Kingfisher.

Aston, Dianne Hutts. 2007. *A Seed Is Sleepy*. New York: Chronicle Books.

Avison, Brigid. 2003. *I Wonder Why I Blink: And Other Questions About My Body*. Boston: Kingfisher.

Baylor, Byrd. 1997. *The Other Way to Listen*. New York: Aladdin.

Brandt, Deanna. 1998. *Bird Log Kids: A Kid's Journal to Record Their Birding Experiences*. Cambridge, MA: Adventure Publications.

Bunting, Eve. 1999. *Butterfly House*. New York: Scholastic.

———. 2003. *Anna's Table*. Minocqua, WI: NorthWord Press.

Carle, Eric. 2005. *A House for Hermit Crab*. New York: Aladdin.

Charman, Andrew. 2003. *I Wonder Why Trees Have Leaves: And Other Questions About Plants*. Boston: Kingfisher.

Christian, Peggy. 2008. *If You Find a Rock*. San Anselmo, CA: Sandpiper Press.

Dewitt, Lynda. 1993. *What Will the Weather Be?* Let's-Read-and-Find-Out Science series, Stage 2. New York: HarperCollins.

DK Publishing. 2006. *First Nature Encyclopedia*. London: DK Publishing.

———. 2008. *First Science Encyclopedia*. New York: DK Publishing.

Dorros, Arthur. 1990. *Feel the Wind*. Let's-Read-and-Find-Out Science series, Stage 2. New York: HarperCollins.

Dunbar, Joyce. 1991. *Why Is the Sky Up?* Boston: Houghton Mifflin.

Ganeri, Anita. 2003. *I Wonder Why the Sea Is Salty: And Other Questions About the Oceans*. Boston: Kingfisher.

———. 2003. *I Wonder Why the Wind Blows: And Other Questions About Our Planet.* Boston: Kingfisher.

George, Kristine O'Connell. 1998. *Old Elm Speaks: Tree Poems.* New York: Clarion Books.

Gibbons, Gail. 1990. *Tell Me, Tree: All About Trees for Kids.* Boston: Little, Brown.

Grindley, Sally. 2006. *Why Is the Sky Blue?* Atlanta: Andersen Press.

Heiligman, Deborah. 1996. *From Caterpillar to Butterfly.* New York: HarperCollins.

Hulbert, Jay, and Sid Kantor. 1994. *Armando Asked, "Why?"* Portsmouth, NH: Heinemann.

Jenkins, Priscilla Belz. 1995. *A Nest Full of Eggs.* Let's-Read-and-Find-Out Science series, Stage 1. New York: HarperCollins.

Jordan, Helene J. 1992. *How a Seed Grows.* Let's-Read-and-Find-Out Science series, Stage 1. New York: HarperCollins.

Kramer, David C. 1989. *Animals in the Classroom: Selection, Care, and Observations.* Boston: Addison-Wesley.

Lember, Barbara Hirsch. 1997. *The Shell Book.* New York: Houghton Mifflin.

Martin, Bill, Jr. 1988. *Listen to the Rain.* New York: Henry Holt.

Maynard, Christopher. 2003. *I Wonder Why Planes Have Wings: And Other Questions About Transportation.* Boston: Kingfisher.

McCloskey, Robert. 1989. *Time of Wonder*. New York: Puffin.

McDonald, Megan. 1993. *Is This a House for Hermit Crab*? New York: Scholastic.

O'Neill, Amanda. 2003. *I Wonder Why Spiders Spin Webs: And Other Questions About Creepy-Crawlies*. Boston: Kingfisher.

———. 2003. *I Wonder Why Snakes Shed Their Skin: And Other Questions About Reptiles*. Boston: Kingfisher.

Pfeffer, Wendy. 1996. *What's It Like to Be a Fish?* Let's-Read-and-Find-Out Science series, Stage 1. New York: HarperCollins.

Ripley. Catherine. 1996. *Why Do Stars Twinkle? And Other Nighttime Questions*. Toronto: Maple Tree Press.

———. 1997. *Why Is the Sky Blue? And Other Outdoor Questions*. Toronto: Maple Tree Press.

———. 2004. *Why? The Best Ever Question and Answer Book About Nature, Science, and the World Around You*. Toronto: Maple Tree Press.

Rockwell, Anne. 2008. *Clouds*. Let's-Read-and-Find-Out Science series, Stage 1. New York: HarperCollins.

Roemer, Heidi. 2009. *Whose Nest Is This?* Minocqua, WI: NorthWord Press.

Serafini, Frank. 2008. *Looking Closely Inside the Garden*. Tonawanda, NY: Kids Can Press.

Shannon, David. 1998. *No, David!* New York: Scholastic.

Showers, Paul. 1961. *The Listening Walk*. New York: HarperCollins.

Silver, Donald M. 1993. *One Small Square: Backyard*. New York: Learning Triangle Press.

Slade, Suzanne. 2008. *From Caterpillar to Butterfly: Following the Life Cycle*. Minneapolis, MN: Picture Window Books.

Taylor, Barbara. 2002. *I Wonder Why Soap Makes Bubbles: And Other Questions About Science*. Boston: Kingfisher.

————. 2003. *I Wonder Why Zippers Have Teeth: And Other Questions About Inventions*. Boston: Kingfisher.

————. 2006. *I Wonder Why the Sun Rises: And Other Questions About Time and Seasons*. Boston: Kingfisher.

Book Series

DK Publishing: DK's First Reference Series

HarperCollins: Let's-Read-and-Find-Out Science: Stages 1 & 2
Sample titles include:
Bugs Are Insects
From Caterpillar to Butterfly
From Seed to Pumpkin
From Tadpole to Frog
How a Seed Grows
A Tree Is a Plant
What Lives in a Shell?

What's It Like to Be a Fish?

Where Are the Night Animals?

Where Do Chicks Come From?

Houghton Mifflin: Backyard Books

Vicki Cobb: Discover Your Five Senses (*Your Tongue Can Tell, Follow Your Nose, Perk Up Your Ears, Open Your Eyes, Feeling Your Way*)

Chapter Two
Nonfiction Writing from the Heart

A child's world is fresh and new and beautiful, full of wonder and excitement. It is our misfortune that for most of us that clear-eyed vision, that true instinct for what is beautiful and awe-inspiring, is dimmed and even lost before we reach adulthood. If I had an influence with the good fairy who is supposed to preside over all children I should ask that her gift to each child in the world would be a sense of wonder so indestructible that it would last through life.

~ Rachel Carson

Introduction

"What are your seven greatest wonders?" Lewis Thomas was asked when he was invited to join several of the world's greatest thinkers at a dinner. Thomas describes his seven wonders in his brilliant book *Late Night Thoughts on Listening to Mahler's Ninth Symphony* (1983). As I was reading Thomas's book one morning, I asked my son, "What do *you* wonder about?"

He looked at me, incredulous. "Mom, I wonder about everything!"

I persisted. "Like what kinds of things do you wonder about?"

"I wonder how the whole world works," he said.

Then I asked if he would write down his seven biggest wonders. Here is what he wrote:

1. I wonder about the world—how things, plants, oceans, space work.
2. I wonder about gravity—why everything has to fall down.
3. I wonder about the moon—if it has aliens on it.
4. I wonder about animals and their defenses.
5. I wonder about how electricity and wires work.
6. I wonder about the sea monster in Scotland.
7. I wonder about everything.

I realized then that his questions reflected the topics of books he chooses to read as well. He selects books at the library about the Loch Ness monster (question 6) and books about animals and their defenses (question 4). He loves to browse through *The Way Things Work* by David Macaulay (1988; question 1). He flips through the pages trying to assimilate words, pictures, and diagrams and is completely absorbed. His questions are a rudder guiding his learning.

Jen and I believe that we need to lay the groundwork for creating lifelong questioners, but it's also essential to set the foundation for nonfiction writing. Young children need to know that nonfiction writing is varied, but at the core of all nonfiction writing is often a question, an observation, a passion fermenting in the author's mind and heart.

A note about age groups: When Jen and I began exploring creating a wonder environment (as described in Chapter 1), she was a kindergarten teacher. The following year Jen became a first-grade teacher, and the work we describe in Chapters 2 and 3 is with first graders.

Nonfiction Writing from the Heart

1. What Are Your Three Wonders?

2. Wonder Boxes

3. Heart Wonders

4. Books of Wonder: Writing Nonfiction from the Heart

Curricular and State Standards Connections to Chapter 2

✓ Stimulate curiosity

✓ Learn through inquiry

✓ Learn through observation

✓ Gather data through senses

✓ Stimulate imagination and creativity

✓ Respond with wonderment and awe

✓ Find or determine answers to questions derived from curiosity about everyday experiences

✓ Recognize and solve problems through observation and active exploration

1. What Are Your Three Wonders?

Judge others by their questions rather than by their answers.

~ Voltaire

I was born on Friday the thirteenth, so I've always considered the number thirteen to be a lucky number. I'm intrigued that many hotels and apartment buildings skip the thirteenth floor, and go from twelve to fourteen. In one hotel in New York City, the elevator stops on floor twelve-and-a-half instead

Resource Materials

✓ *Where Do Balloons Go?* by Jamie Lee Curtis

✓ *The Wise Old Woman and Her Secret* by Eve Merriam

✓ Wonder sheet (*see Appendix*) or index cards

✓ Clipboards

✓ Large chart and easel

of thirteen. "Doesn't everybody know that floor number fourteen is really number thirteen?" my son once asked me. One of my wonders had always been why the number thirteen is considered so unlucky. Another author was wondering the same thing and published a book called *Thirteen: A Journey into the Number* (Cott 1996). This book helped me answer my question, which has a lot of historic and mythological lore surrounding it. In this book, one of my wonders was answered.

Many books have been written by exploring a question. Sue Bender wrote *Plain and Simple: A Woman's Journey into the Amish* (1991) because she noticed that there was no difference between the everyday and the sacred in the Amish community. She asked the questions, What really matters? Is there another way to live a good life?

John McPhee wrote a book entitled *Oranges* (1966) because he noticed that the orange juice he drank every morning was a different color depending on the time of year, and he wondered why. His book explores the origin of orange juice as well as current orange juice production.

Whether our wonders are grounded in personal experiences or scientific fact, we all wonder.

Jen and I wanted to share Lewis Thomas's wonder idea and ask children to jot down their wonders to prepare them for writing about their wonders through nonfiction writing.

The children in Jen's first-grade class were gathered on the rug as Jen sat in her reading spot, the rocking chair. She made eye contact with each child until they settled down and were ready to listen. "Today, I have something very special to share with you," she told them.

"I hope it's writer's workshop!" Luke blurted, his hands together in a prayer position. Jen smiled and moved on.

"Today, I have two books to share with you," she said. "The first one is by a writer named Lewis Thomas, and I'll just tell you about the book he wrote. It's called *Late Night Thoughts on Listening to Mahler's Ninth Symphony*. Whew! What a long title!" Jen then told the children the story about Thomas's seven wonders.

"The second book is called *Where Do Balloons Go?* by Jamie Lee Curtis. The author always wondered where balloons went when people let go of them, so she wrote a book about it."

Jordan whispered to Annie, "It's like wondering where our guinea pig went." (One of our class guinea pigs had escaped the week before, and the children were sure that he was out having grand adventures!)

Jen read the book and everyone sat cross-legged, listening intently. After she finished reading, she told the class, "Just like Lewis Thomas and Jamie Lee Curtis, I've put down three things I wonder about on this chart."

Jen wrote on a white chart:

1. What do ants do under the ground?

"This is a wonder that came from watching my son Will watch ants one day," Jen explained. "Sometimes a wonder can come from observing something like when Will taught me to really look at the ants. Then I began to wonder, what do ants do under the ground?"

2. What makes a best friend a best friend?

"I have lots of friends, but no one is like my friend Tiffany, and I was wondering just what makes a best friend a best friend. This is a wonder that comes from my heart."

3. What makes people's hair grow in different colors?

"This is a wonder that I've wondered my whole life. I'm thinking that some of you probably have a wonder that you've carried for a long time too." Jen shared with her students the roots of her wonders to model the ways in which questions can be inspired.

"That's what you're going to be doing today," she told the class. "You're going to think about what your three wonders are just like Lewis Thomas did. Why don't you close your eyes and begin to think about some of the things you wonder about."

After a few minutes, Jen asked the children to turn their attention back to her. They opened their eyes and thrust their hands in the air to share their wonders. After each child shared one wonder Jen whispered, "I'd like you to go to your book spots now, lie down on the floor, and just let your mind think, 'What do I wonder about?' 'What are my top three wonders?'"

Jen turned off the bright lights, so the classroom was lit by strings of Christmas lights. The kids settled into places around the room. Kelly laid on her stomach, elbows on the floor, propping her head in her hands. Bella was on her back, hands behind her head, staring up at the lights. Some children had their eyes closed; others looked up at the ceiling. Annie counted her three wonders slowly on her fingers.

After several minutes, Jen interrupted with a whisper, "Now, tiptoe to your seats and write down your three wonders."

She gave each child three index cards—one for each wonder. A few boys yelled out, "Sweet! Awesome!" Jen and I walked around the room and glanced over the children's shoulders. We stopped and crouched down at a few desks and asked the children to share their wonders. Luke wrote,

1. How do leaves change in the fall?

2. How does the rain go in the sky?

3. How do they make snow?

Daisy wrote, "How do you make chains? How do they make sweetness?" At the corner table, two boys were engaged in an intense discussion about God based on a wonder, Who is God? Is he a spirit?

The children were asking a range of questions, from deeply spiritual and philosophical questions about the natural world to more personal questions like, "Why can't I get my ears pierced?"

Griffin's two wonders were

1. How does the avocado seed get put in the avocado?

2. How do rain clouds get filled with water?

Some of the children were beginning to explore their questions already. Griffin elaborated on his question about the avocado seed by explaining to his tablemates what he meant. "I mean, how *do* they put seeds in fruit? To put the seeds in you have to mush the fruit and strawberries. And strawberries aren't mushed up." As he spoke, he gestured dramatically, holding his hands out in a question pose, shrugging his shoulders.

The atmosphere in the room was magical. Every child was actively engaged in thinking, discussing, and writing about their wonders.

After fifteen minutes, Jen said, "You all did a fantastic job with your wonderings. Maybe we can help one another explore these questions. Come to the rug with your wonders."

When the children were seated in a circle on the rug, Jen said, "Read over your wonders and choose one that you think will be the most interesting to think about and maybe even try to find an explanation for." The children glanced at their papers and hands shot up. Jen first called on Bella.

Bella read, "How does the sun get so hot?"

Jen asked the students if any of them had any explanations or thoughts to contribute about Bella's wonder. Leo raised his hand and said, "A million years ago there was a hot planet explosion and one of the planets turned into the sun. It got so hot."

Bella interrupted, "I saw in a book that the sun was on fire."

"Maybe the sun is so hot because it's fire!" Kelly said.

"Bella, maybe you can take this wonder home with you. Think about it some more. Talk to someone in your family, and see if you can add to your explanation," Jen said. "Also, if you have the book where you saw the sun on fire, you could look at that again as well."

At the end of sharing, Jen asked students to choose one of their wonders to say out loud. Jen wrote down all these wonders. When they realized that their collective list sounded like a list poem, they displayed it on a chart in the room:

We Wonder

I wonder why elephants have their babies not in eggs.
I wonder why there were dinosaurs at all.
I wonder if the universe ever stops.
I wonder how New York City was built.
I wonder how butterflies' wings are created.
I wonder how people are made.

I wonder how locks are made.
I wonder how bricks were made.
I wonder why the sun goes down at night.
I wonder why the moon only comes out at night and not day.
I wonder how many years dinosaurs lived.
I wonder how come snakes can't close their eyes at night.
I wonder how car wheels can make a whole car move.
I wonder where sweetness comes from.
I wonder how snakes shed their skin from inside out.

In the days following this lesson, the children shared more of their questions.

Jen's Reflection

The idea about ants came from a walk I took with my two-year-old son and his fascination with an ant pile we saw along the way. Try to see the world through young eyes, and the questions will begin to flow. You will also want to start paying attention to the books in your classroom library, school library, and public library that ask and answer questions. Debbie Miller's book Reading with Meaning (2002) recommends a great book called The Wise Woman and Her Secret by Eve Merriam (1999), which could also be used to introduce this idea of wonder. The kids were naturally full of wonders, so getting them to come up with ideas was easy. For kids that may have trouble, send them to the observation window to look outside. Once they start thinking of wonders, they won't be able to stop.

2. Wonder Boxes

Anything under the sun is beautiful if you have the vision —
it is the seeing of the thing that makes it so.

~ Nathaniel Hawthorne

Debbie Miller writes in her brilliant book *Reading with Meaning,* "Children everywhere know that the secret of wisdom is to be curious about the world, to open up their senses and see, hear, taste, touch, and smell life's treasures. Giving children time to explore their world, ask questions, and pursue those questions that matter to them most lets them know I value their curiosity outside the classroom as well as inside. My job is to continue to nurture their wonder and work to awaken my own" (2002, 135).

> **Resource Materials**
>
> ✓ Index cards
> ✓ Small recipe boxes (or any box that fit index cards)
>
> OR
>
> ✓ Small envelopes
> ✓ Large envelopes

The children in Jen's class arrived in the morning excited and brimming with more questions. They needed a permanent place to write down their wonders so they could return to them later and explore them in writing.

Jen gathered them on the rug for a mini-lesson. She wanted to discuss with the children the idea of keeping their questions in wonder boxes. We borrowed the idea of wonder boxes from Debbie Miller's book about her first-grade classroom.

Jen told the children, "Now that you've been thinking about so many questions and writing them down so you won't forget them, we're going to start something very special today. Because you have so many questions, and you'll want to keep them with you, everyone will get a wonder box to keep their wonders in."

They were thrilled. They smiled; some clapped their hands, and a couple whispered, "Thank you." Their excitement was palpable.

The wonder boxes were shiny metallic silver, gold, and red boxes that could fit paper the size of index cards. As Jen called their names, each child chose one. She then stuck typed name labels on the front of each wonder box.

"This is where you can keep your wonders. So during the day, or at home, if you think of a wonder, just grab an index card, write down your wonder, and keep it in your wonder box."

As the children packed up for lunch, more wonders popped into their heads, and they grabbed more index cards to write them down. As they lined up and walked out the door, we could still hear them speaking their wonders aloud as their voices trailed away.

Jen's Reflection

The wonder boxes are an amazing way to funnel kids' questions and wonders. Naturally, children will have a great deal of enthusiasm for anything new, so having a place for kids to store their questions and excitement is not only perfect for the kids but keeps you sane and organized.

If you can't find boxes to keep the wonder cards in, then consider storing wonder cards in small envelopes—just the right size to fit index cards—and then put the small envelopes into a larger envelope labeled "My Wonders."

---

3. Heart Wonders

The best and most beautiful things in the world cannot be seen nor touched but are felt in the heart.

~ *Helen Keller*

Resource Materials

✓ Easel and large chart
✓ Wonder boxes

Teeth are brushed. Pajamas are on. Stuffed bears are positioned all around. Leo and I snuggle in and begin our bedtime reading: stories, books, and poems. Tonight I'll read a book that Leo has heard many times before, *Mama, Do You Love Me?* by Barbara Joosse. I start reading as Leo snuggles closer.

"Mama, do you love me? Yes, I do, Dear one. How much...?"

How many times had Leo asked that same question of me? When I answer, it's always from my heart, and not something I can research in a book.

We wanted to teach kids that nonfiction writing begins with a question, an observation, or an interest that the author is passionate about and can be answered by either thinking carefully about what we believe or by researching and learning what we don't know.

Jen began her mini-lesson, "We watched you yesterday as you wrote down your wonders and put them in your wonder boxes. You all wonder about so much. Did anyone go home yesterday and think of more wonders to put in your wonder boxes?" Most hands go up.

Jen wrote "Different Kinds of Wonders" at the top of a chart. On the left-hand side, she wrote "Heart Wonders," and drew a little heart next to the words. On the right-hand side, she wrote "Research Wonders" and drew a book, a person, a computer, and an eye (symbols of different ways children can research their questions). She left the middle of the chart blank for another kind of wonder that the children might come up with.

"Now that you've written so many wonders, I bet you're asking yourselves the same question I'm asking myself, 'How can I go about finding the answers to all these wonders?' Well, you can explore your wonders in many different ways," Jen said. "One way you can explore your wonder is by just thinking about it. Like my question, 'What makes a best friend a best friend?' I need to use both my heart and my mind to try to answer that question. I wouldn't necessarily go to the library or to a computer to look for the answer. I might ask a few people what they think makes a best friend, but mainly the answer will come from my heart. So I've written on the chart "Heart Wonders," and I'm going to put this question there because I'll answer this question from my heart."

The children listened as Jen continued. "And what about my question, 'What goes on under an ant pile?' Is that a question that I can answer from my heart, or should I go to the library and find a book about ants? Or maybe I can see what ants do under an ant pile with my own eyes. Maybe I can observe them by digging in the dirt a little. So I might look in a book or try to find the answer with my own eyes, or I could also do some research on the computer. Where do you think I should put that question? Under 'Heart Wonder' or 'Research Wonder'?"

Most children said in unison, "Research," although Shawn yelled out "Heart!"

Jen asked Shawn, "Why do you think it's from my heart?"

He said, "Because I watch ants, and I know in my heart what they do."

"Today, you'll be taking your wonders out of your wonder boxes and putting them into two piles: one for heart wonders—questions that you can answer with your heart and minds—and one for research wonders—questions that you'll want to look up in books or on the computer. You can even draw a heart at the top of your heart wonders index cards, and you could draw a picture of an eye at the top of your research wonders index cards to show that you'll use your eyes to look in a book or observe something to find an answer for that question."

Jen looked at Griffin and asked, "Do you remember your wonder, 'What makes a family?' Well, I'm wondering if you would list that wonder under a "Heart Wonder" or a "Research Wonder"? Griffin thought for awhile and said, "Heart Wonder."

Jen agreed. "That wonder is not a fact that you could find in a book. People might have written in a book what they believe in their hearts about families, but the answer to that question will come from your heart." Jen taped Griffin's index card to the chart under "Heart Wonder."

We sent the children back to their tables to reread their written wonders and to think through whether their wonders were heart or research wonders.

As we walked around the room looking over the children's shoulders, they sorted their questions into two piles. Jen crouched down next to Caroline, who had two piles stacked neatly on her desk. In her research wonders pile were questions like, "I wonder how smelly markers are made?" "I wonder how seeds are made?" "I wonder how books are made?" Caroline understood that she would be able to research these wonders using books, magazines, computers, or observation. But Jen and I were curious why, in her heart wonder pile, she had this question: "How do oceans get made?"

Jen sat down next to her and asked, "I'm curious about your question 'How do oceans get made?' I'm wondering where you think you might find the answer to that question."

Caroline responded, "In my heart."

"So if you go inside your heart, how do you think oceans are made?" Jen asked her.

Caroline says, "From a mystery and water."

Caroline had categorized as a heart wonder a question that most of us assume would be explored through research. To Caroline, the ocean is a big, mysterious, powerful place. To us, that mystery has faded somewhat with knowledge and experience. Caroline wasn't asking her question from a scientist's perspective; perhaps she wasn't even aware that a scientific explanation existed. Instead, she was asking the question from the perspective of a child who looks at the world with wonder.

Jen stopped the class in mid-workshop and asked whether anyone was having trouble choosing a pile for their questions. Griffin raised his hand and said, "All my invented ones. I'm not sure where they should go." Jen asked him what he meant by "invented ones."

"Like, 'Who invented holidays?'" he said. "And 'Who invented Halloween?' 'Who invented clothes?' I'm not sure where they go."

"Well, maybe we should have a separate pile for those questions we're not sure how to answer," Jen told the class. "Maybe you can put a question mark on those questions you're not sure of where to put."

Jen then handed out dividers to separate the children's wonder index cards within their wonder boxes. She asked them to draw on the tabs a heart for heart wonders, an eye for research wonders, and a question mark for wonders they weren't sure of.

The children's heart wonders piles included these questions:

Where does magic come from? (Hunter)

Why do we have a family? (Joseph)

Why do I love my dog? (Austin)

Rachel Carson writes, "If facts are the seeds that later produce knowledge and wisdom, then the emotions and the impressions of the senses are the fertile soil in which the seeds must grow" (1965, 56).

Students' heart wonders were based on emotions and impressions, which would plant the seeds for exploring questions. It didn't matter whether the distinctions were exact but rather that the children understood that there are various ways to go about exploring questions.

Later, as Jen and I read all the cards, we realized that the children who were more emotional and sensitive tended to have more cards in heart wonders piles, and those children who were more literal tended to put all of their questions into the research wonders pile.

Jen's Reflection

As I watched Georgia confer with my students, I realized that the most important questions we asked were, "Why do you think this is a heart wonder?" And, "Why do you think that is a research wonder?" I was surprised and assured to realize that the kids knew and could explain their decisions. Also, if you listen closely, their answers will give you an insight into the kind of wonderers they are. Some kids are very enlightened and almost spiritual about their wonders; others are more grounded and literal in their thinking. Knowing how your kids think and believe will help you guide them as they begin to find their passions and begin their writing.

4. Books of Wonder: Writing Nonfiction from the Heart

Fill your paper with the breathings of your heart.

~ William Wordsworth

Resource Materials

✓ *Wilfred Gordon McDonald Partridge* by Mem Fox

✓ *Mama, Do You Love Me?* by Barbara M. Joosse

✓ *Is This a House for Hermit Crab?* by Megan McDonald

When I was a girl, I shared my wonder of the stars with my grandfather. In the summer, he set up a telescope on the front porch, and I saw the moon transformed from a lovely distant object to a place filled with craters, shadows, and holes. At ninety-two, my grandfather's eyesight deteriorated, so I read books to him about astronomy as he fell asleep in the late afternoon sun on the screened porch.

I had so many questions about stars from my nightly gazing into the telescope and from the books my grandfather and I read together. I wondered how far away the stars were from one another. I wondered whether each star was a distant galaxy. I wondered about black holes. I wondered whether there was life on other stars. I traced the constellations with my fingers as I lay on the field and wondered how ancient people ever came up with the names Orion's Belt or the Big and Little Dippers.

These questions about the stars still seep into my writing and have even become the subject of a few poems. Here's one:

Stars

Connect the dots. Make sky stories:
Taurus the Bull; Aries the Ram;
Leo the Lion; the Big Dipper —
Tales stitched onto an endless night.

Find a star. Sing sky songs:
Twinkle, twinkle little star . . .
When you wish upon a star . . .
Melodies sung in a hushed night.

Just as my poem "Stars" was inspired by my impressions of looking at the night sky, we wanted the children to write their nonfiction pieces inspired by their impressions and emotions first. We hoped that starting with heart wonders would teach them to write their research nonfiction pieces with more voice and expression.

We gathered the first graders together and placed a basket of books next to us. We wanted to show them children's books in which the author's wonder inspired the book and books that had the wonder and questions incorporated into the text. Some of the books we shared were fiction picture books, and some were nonfiction books. We began by modeling two popular pictures books.

"Today I have a basket of books on my lap. We're going to be writing books this week based on one of our heart wonders," Jen told the children one morning. "I'm going to read a book that you know already, but this time, as you listen to the story, I'd like you to notice that the character asks a heart wonder. Do you remember *Wilfrid Gordon McDonald Partridge* by Mem Fox?"

There is a resounding "Yes" from the kids.

"Does anyone remember what question in the book Wilfrid Gordon McDonald Partridge tries to answer?"

No takers.

"Let me read you a part of that book again."

> *"What's a memory?" asked Wilfrid Gordon. He was always asking questions.*
>
> *"It is something you remember," said his father.*
>
> *But Wilfrid Gordon wanted to know more, so he called on Mrs Jordan who played the organ.*
>
> *"What's a memory?" he asked.*
>
> *"Something warm, my child, something warm."*

"Remember," Jen said, "Wilfrid Gordon goes around and asks different people the same question, and they all give him a different answer. When Mrs. Jordan answers with 'Something warm, my child, something warm,' the answer didn't come from a book, but it came from her heart and experiences in her life.

"It's kind of like when I asked the question, 'What makes a best friend a best friend?' There's no one answer, and if I asked each one of you that question, everyone would have a different answer. Here are more heart wonder books."

Jen held up *Mama, Do You Love Me?* by Barbara M. Joosse, *What If the Zebras Lost Their Stripes?* by John Reitano, and *How Do Dinosaurs Say Goodnight?* by Jane Yolen. "In fact, there's a whole basket of books here that answer questions more as a poet would rather than a scientist. Some books of wonder give us information and facts but are written like poetry, such as *Is This a House for Hermit Crab?* The title is a question about where hermit crabs live, and the question is answered in a poetic way but is based on the author's observations and information about hermit crabs":

> *Hermit Crab was forever growing too big for the house on his back. It was time to find a new house. He crawled up out of the water looking for something to hide in, where he would be safe from the pricklepine fish.*
>
> *He stepped along the shore by the sea, in the sand . . . scritch-scratch, scritch-scratch . . . until he came to a rock.*
>
> *Is this a house for hermit crab?*

"Today, you're going to begin writing the kind of book of wonder where you write it from your heart."

Jen continued, "So today, watch as I get ready to choose one of my heart wonders (the ones I drew a heart beside), and then I'll write out what I think. I'm going to choose 'What makes a best friend?' I am going to first write on this sheet that will help my thinking":

- Is it because we like the same things?

- Is it because we have known each other for a long time?

"After I've brainstormed some ideas, then I'll get my writing book and write some of my ideas into my book."

The kids nod and seem eager to get started.

"I'd like you to start by looking in your wonder boxes," Jen said. "Choose a heart wonder you would like to explore today in your writing. Pick the one that's most interesting to you, the one you think you could write most about. Once you have it, turn to the person next to you and whisper what your book of wonder will be about and some of the ideas you have in exploring your heart wonder."

We watched as each child enthusiastically discussed one of their wonders.

After a few minutes, Jen asked for attention again. "Okay, writers, let's get started," she said. "You might want to start by writing your wonder as the title of your book, and then use your thoughts to write your own book of wonder. I have sheets here for you to explore your questions on. Then when you are ready, you can start writing your book from your heart."

Jen wrote on chart paper, "Please Choose One of Your Heart Wonders to Explore Today."

We created a "think" sheet for those who needed to plan their thoughts out before they wrote (see Figure 2.1).

Figure 2.1

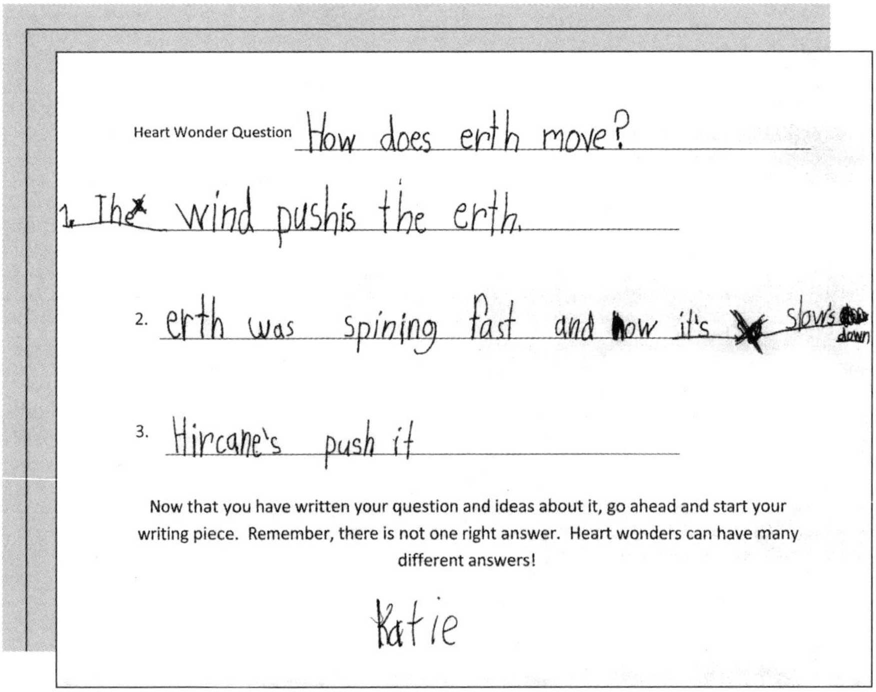

Heart Wonder Question How does erth move?

1. The wind pushis the erth.

2. erth was spining fast and now it's slows down

3. Hircane's push it

Now that you have written your question and ideas about it, go ahead and start your writing piece. Remember, there is not one right answer. Heart wonders can have many different answers!

Katie

Katie's heart wonder question think sheet

The clean-up song played softly in the background as the kids packed their heart wonders back into their wonder boxes and headed to the rug for share time.

Noelle sat up tall in the writer's chair as she waited for the song to end and her listeners to get quiet. She had worked on writing out her answer to her heart question, "Where did God come from?"

"Go ahead, Noelle. I think they're ready for you," I said softly as the rest of the class settled on the rug.

Noelle began, "Who made the world? Who invented stars? Is it the wind? I think it's love."

"What do you think?" Noelle asked the class. And she put her piece down and looked at the kids staring up at her. Well, of course, that was an invitation that couldn't be ignored and hands went right up.

Daniela was first. "Maybe someone gave birth to him? Oh, I don't know." She giggled and started second-guessing herself. Noelle knew just what to do, and before I could jump in to reassure Daniela, Noelle had turned to the page in her story about someone coming before him and said, "See Daniela, I thought that same thing on this page."

Allison was next, "Maybe God made himself?"

"Nope, God is power and love. That is what my parents told me," Margo firmly stated.

Julia couldn't help but agree and added, "Yeah, he is a spirit all right, but if we can't see him, how do we know?" Her eyes searched out an answer from all of us.

Jamie's quiet voice came through just at that moment. "How do we know, Julia? We all just know." A few seconds of quiet followed as eighteen heads nodded in agreement. Then just as quickly, seemingly satisfied with that answer, the kids got up, and we headed out to recess.

Their nonfiction heart wonder pieces were written with amazingly little structure except for the think sheet and modeling, but the kids had a lot of passion and enthusiasm for exploring wonder.

Jen and I can't imagine a time when the children didn't ask questions, have wonders, and explore answers. Here is an example of a book of wonder (see Figure 2.2):

Figure 2.2

Date: 5/31/06

I Woder Were is hevin

Written by:

by kendall

Were is hevin?

Hevin is up hiye.

Hevin is down lawe.

And hevin is bothe

Sids.

come up now.

hevin is evrywere.

Hevin is were you go

When you die.

It's sad when you go

to hevin.

bey Pepole that die!

Evrybaty go's to hevin

Inthen you tern into

Sumone els.

Kendall's wonder book: "I wonder where is heaven."

Jen's Reflection

Our hope was that the students' voices would transfer into their nonfiction research pieces and that this kind of writing would become a kind of "mulling over" of what they thought and believed. When kids became stuck, we encouraged them to ask their fellow classmates what they thought about the question and to include some of those answers in their writing pieces.

One tip that I gave writers in my mini-lesson and when I conferred with them was to make sure they asked a question and then tried to answer it.

Books for Nonfiction Writing
from the Heart

Curtis, Jamie Lee. 2000. *Where Do Balloons Go? An Uplifting Mystery*. New York: HarperCollins.

Dunbar, Joyce. 1991. *Why Is the Sky Up?* Boston: Houghton Mifflin.

Fox, Mem. 1989. *Wilfrid Gordon McDonald Partridge*. La Jolla, CA: Kane/Miller.

Hopkins, Lee Bennett. 2009. *Sky Magic*. New York: Dutton Children's Books.

Hulbert, Jay, and Sid Kantor. 1990. *Armando Asked, "Why?"* Portsmouth, NH: Heinemann Library.

Joosse, Barbara M. 1998. *Mama, Do You Love Me?* New York: Chronicle Books.

Martin, Bill, Jr. 1967. *Brown Bear, Brown Bear, What Do You See?* New York: Henry Holt.

McDonald, Megan. 1990. *Is This a House for a Hermit Crab?* New York: Orchard Books.

Melmed, Laura Krauss. 1993. *The First Song Ever Sung*. New York: Lothrop Lee & Shepard.

Merriam, Eve. 1999. *The Wise Woman and Her Secret*. New York: Aladdin.

Muth, Jon. 2002. *The Three Questions*. New York: Scholastic.

Oppenheim, Joanne. 1996. *Have You Seen Bugs?* New York: Scholastic.

Oppenheim, Shulamith. 2000. *What Is the Full Moon Full Of?* New York: Yearling.

Pitcher, Caroline. 2000. *Are You Spring?* New York: Dorling Kindersley.

Reitano, John. 1998. *What If the Zebras Lost Their Stripes?* Mahwah, NJ: Paulist Press.

Yolen, Jane. 2000. *How Do Dinosaurs Say Goodnight?* New York: Blue Sky Press.

Chapter Three

Nonfiction Research
Wonder Writing

I sincerely believe that for the child . . . it is not half so important to know as to feel.
If facts are the seeds that later produce knowledge and wisdom, then the
emotions and the impressions of the senses are the fertile soil in which the seeds
must grow. The years of early childhood are the time to prepare the soil.

~ Rachel Carson

Introduction

Wonder and curiosity are the doors into the world of writing for many authors. Shelley Harwayne writes in her brilliant book, *Novel Perspectives*, "When I walk down the street with my friends who take their writing seriously, they are always asking questions. Writers are curious about things and always eager to find answers to their questions" (2005, 61). Harwayne quotes an excerpt from Arlene J. Chai's novel *The Last Time I Saw Mother*:

> *"Why?" is a word children learn early in life. And it was a word I continued to use long after most children had moved on to other words.*
>
> *The word itself creates an empty sensation. Try saying it now. "Why?" Notice how your tongue touches nothing when you form the word with your mouth. Feel the gap, the space inside your mouth, that it creates. The air. It is a place that needs filling. It is missing an answer. (61)*

I wrote *Creatures of Earth, Sea, and Sky: Animal Poems* (1992) after I researched numerous animals and insects and realized that many were on the endangered species list. I ended the book with a list poem of questions.

Will We Ever See?

> *Will we ever see a tiger again,*
> *stalking its prey with shining eyes?*
> *Will we see the giant orangutan*
> *inspecting its mate for fleas?*
> *Or a California condor*
> *feeding on the side of a hill?*
> *Or a whooping crane*
> *walking softly through a salty marsh?*
> *Or hear the last of the blue whales*
> *singing its sad song under deep water?*

Being curious is a writer's stance. We write from what we don't know toward understanding.

Young children live in a world where they're trying to figure out how the world works. Questions are a doorway into writing for many children, especially struggling students. Often we begin teaching nonfiction writing by asking children to simply follow a template and then research and record facts that they've gathered from books and other resources without first guiding them in how to assimilate the information they've gathered or how to write nonfiction.

Before we engage primary children in writing research-based nonfiction, Jen and I knew that first they needed to feel comfortable and fluent in writing about their beliefs, wonders, and thoughts. The lack of that comfort is why many children (including Jen and me) were tempted to copy facts for research reports from encyclopedias and other books. We were not comfortable with the genre, hadn't developed our voice as writers of nonfiction, didn't know how to assimilate information we learned about our topics, and weren't encouraged to write what we believed or thought about a topic. We first asked children to explore their wonders through writing from their hearts and minds, and then we wove the research process into the wonder of the week center and Friday pondering time.

We realized that the classroom environment needed to foster the kind of thinking in which we wanted to immerse kids. This meant setting up wonder centers in the classroom to prepare the children for nonfiction writing and thinking. Our goal was not only to get the kids excited about their wonders but also to provide an outlet for a continuous flow of wonders discussed in class.

The children became eager to research their questions using some of the resources we had talked about during our Friday pondering time. Thus, we decided it was time to move on to our second category of wonders—nonfiction writing: research wonders.

We discovered that the kids were capable of creating nonfiction research pieces that were unique, rich in voice, and written with an audience in mind. Voice in particular can be hard to teach to young writers, especially in nonfiction research writing, but by prefacing nonfiction writing with the wonder work ahead of time, developing voice felt like a natural progression.

Nonfiction Research Wonder Writing

1. Exploring Nonfiction Books: Sorting and Cataloguing
2. Exploring Nonfiction Books: Structures and Features
3. Getting Started: Choosing Research Wonder Topics
4. Nonfiction Writing: Trying On Topics
5. Nonfiction Writing: Creating a Table of Contents
6. Nonfiction Writing: Designing Chapters
7. Exploring and Researching Questions
8. Exploring and Researching Questions: Inferring
9. Exploring and Researching Questions: Ask an Expert
10. Nonfiction Writing: Leads/Beginnings
11. Nonfiction Writing: Wow Words
12. Nonfiction Writing: Other Craft Lessons
    Speaking Directly to the Reader
    Question-Answer Format
13. Nonfiction Writing: Elaboration
14. Nonfiction Writing: Diagrams
15. Writing Partner Revision
16. Editing: Using Word Wall Words
17. Partner Editing: Capitals and Periods
18. Publishing and Celebrating

Curricular and State Standards
Connections to Chapter 3

Thinking

✓ Learn through inquiry

✓ Learn through observation

✓ Respond with wonderment and awe

- ✓ Find or determine answers to questions derived from curiosity about everyday experiences
- ✓ Recognize and solve problems through observation and active exploration

Reading

- ✓ Demonstrate understanding of informational text through generating questions and answering questions
- ✓ Connect informational text to life experiences and prior knowledge
- ✓ Retell important facts from the text
- ✓ Identify the message and information of the text
- ✓ Recognize the characteristics of informational texts
- ✓ Use prior knowledge to interpret meaning and make sense of texts
- ✓ Generate questions about topics of personal interest
- ✓ Know that learning can come from careful observation
- ✓ Ask and answer questions

Writing

- ✓ Conduct research on independent topics of interests by generating ideas and questions. Gather, evaluate, and synthesize data from a variety of sources (observation, artifacts, experts, print, digital, etc.) and write about discoveries.
- ✓ Use prewriting strategies to plan written work
- ✓ Discuss with peers, and write key thoughts and questions
- ✓ Rehearse ideas
- ✓ Write on self-chosen topics
- ✓ Use strategies to draft and revise written work
- ✓ Use nonfiction conventions and craft
- ✓ Craft and revise written work
  - Sharpen the focus
  - Use "wow" words
  - Use interesting leads
  - Use editing conventions

Nonfiction Read-Aloud

During our nonfiction study, Jen's read-alouds were mostly nonfiction texts of various kinds in a variety of genres: factual books, nonfiction big books, heart wonder nonfiction books, poetry, books about questioning and wondering, and magazine articles. We selected texts that modeled the children's interests, experiences, and questions and modeled the kinds of topics about which they might write their nonfiction books. After and during read-alouds, we noticed the children's excitement when they learned about something new or discovered something fascinating. We also pointed out some of the books' features and craft and demonstrated how to read a nonfiction book by highlighting its features, such as table of contents, chapters, glossary, diagrams, and an index. We also taught them about craft and asked them to pay particular attention during the read-aloud for "wow" words, compelling beginnings, a point of view where the author speaks directly to the reader, and the question/answer format. We asked kids to predict answers to questions of what might come on the next page.

Here are some of our favorite nonfiction books to read aloud:

Barry, Frances. 2008. *Little Green Frogs*. Boston: Candlewick Press.

Bayrock, Fiona. 2009. *Bubble Homes and Fish Farts*. Charlestown, MA: Charlesbridge.

Campbell, Sarah C. 2008. *Wolfsnail: A Backyard Predator*. Honesdale, PA: Boyds Mills Press.

Franco, Betsy. 2008. *Bees, Snails, & Peacock Tails: Patterns & Shapes . . . Naturally*. New York: Margaret K. McElderry Books.

Hopkins, Lee Bennett. 1994. *Questions: Poems of Wonder*. New York: HarperTrophy.

Jenkins, Steve. 2008. *Sisters and Brothers: Sibling Relationships in the Animal World*. Boston: Houghton Mifflin.

Macken Early, Jo Ann. 2008. *Flip, Float, Fly! Seeds on the Move*. New York: Holiday House.

Melmed, Laura Krauss. 1993. *The First Song Ever Sung*. New York: Lothrop Lee & Shepard.

Oppenheim, Joanne. 1998. *Have You Seen Bugs?* New York: Scholastic.

Seeger, Laura Vaccaro. 2007. *First the Egg*. New York: Roaring Brook Press.

Singer, Marilyn. 2008. *Eggs*. New York: Holiday House.

Nonfiction Immersion

We immersed kids in nonfiction information books during read-aloud as well as during independent reading time as preparation for their selection of writing topics. We checked out appropriate books from the class and school library, gathered children's magazines like *Zoobooks*, and invited children to browse, study, and absorb the world of nonfiction information books. We watched the children's excitement grow as they flipped through books, lingered over photos, and exclaimed about a new piece of information to their classmates. We placed wonder cards on their desks so that if they came across a wonder about a topic they could jot it down to store in their wonder boxes. As we conferred, we asked, "What are you learning?" and "What did you notice about your book?" We also pointed out some of the texts' features that would help them read the books for information, such as captions, table of contents, and other features that Jen would explain more formally in a mini-lesson. This immersion time helped children get excited about their nonfiction book topics and helped guide their topic selection. It also helped us guide the children's research when we knew which of the children's topics had resources.

1. Exploring Nonfiction Books: Sorting and Cataloguing

A book is a garden, an orchard, a storehouse, a party . . .

~ *Henry Ward Beecher*

Resource Materials

✓ A collection of nonfiction books

✓ Plastic bins for books

✓ Strips of white paper or label stickers for book bin labels

✓ Markers

After we moved recently, my husband and I spent two days sorting and cataloguing our varied and abundant library of books. My husband's method was to make a huge pile of books in the middle of the room from which he selected books from the top of the pile to place on the shelves. This drove me crazy since I had a very different method: I made small stacks of books according to genre and then alphabetized them as I placed them on the shelves. Similarly, I drove him crazy because I often picked up a forgotten book and began to read. Memories rushed back, such as where I was when I first bought the book and how much I loved it. By the end of the two days, all the books were sorted by genre and alphabetized. No matter what method we used, we both rediscovered many wonderful books we would reread.

In Jen's class, I happened to overhear a conversation between two of her students, Louie and Rory. The boys were in a big discussion about snails when I sat down to listen in. Louie was asking Rory what snails eat (apparently, Louie had caught one the night before and put it in a shoebox).

Louie asked with earnestness, "So I caught this really cool snail last night, but I'm afraid if I don't give it something to eat, it is going to die. Do you know what they eat?"

Rory replied, "Um, not sure; maybe bugs or grass?"

Looking a little defeated, Louie ended with, "Great, how am I going to figure this out so it won't die?"

I called Jen over and asked her whether she knew of any books in the classroom library about snails. She said that there was a great book about snails and slugs in the nonfiction section of the classroom.

Jen told Louie, "You know, Louie, we have a great book about snails in our classroom library. You could go and get that, and maybe you can read about what snails eat. Would that help?"

Louie and Rory looked at Jen with great interest and inquiry. "Where is the nonfiction part of our library?" they asked.

Jen looked concerned. She told me she had an idea over the summer before the school year started to organize the classroom library into sections in the room. She hung colorful and bold signs above the sections. "Fiction" was written on a colorful rainbow with clouds hanging down from the ceiling. Below it, the bookshelves were stuffed with bins of books sorted by author and by characters. Across the room, there was a big yellow star suspended up high that said "Nonfiction," and below that were books about dinosaurs, animals, sports, and weather, and wonder books that answered questions, among other things. The tops of the shelves housed the hermit crab, the discovery table objects, and magazines. On the outside of the shelves hung posters of dinosaur facts, a nutrition chart, and different kinds of rocks. Jen had thought that organizing the books would be a great way to get kids to think about different genres of reading and to help them find books easily and quickly on topics they wanted to investigate.

After the conversation with Rory and Louie, Jen decided to ask more of her kids about the classroom library and how useful it was to them. Would they know where to find nonfiction information books about different topics? Did they even know a nonfiction section existed? After a few more conversations, Jen realized that her careful thoughts, planning, and organization were just that. Hers. She knew where to find nonfiction books in the classroom because she had organized them. She knew which topics could be found in a particular section because she was the one that organized it. She felt that her kids really didn't have ownership of the books and the library. She knew it was time to get the kids involved. She had to make the classroom library theirs, not hers.

The next morning as the kids were coming into school they noticed something different. The night before, Jen had taken all of the nonfiction books off the shelves and put them around the classroom on the desks and tables. She knew the students would be curious and that would make them start looking at the books. She was right. As the kids were unpacking, they headed right for the books. The kids were holding up and sharing books like they were brand new to the classroom and hadn't been there right in front of them all year long.

"Oh, cool! Austin, look! Here is a book about the dinosaurs and how big their teeth are," exclaimed Ethan.

"Look at these books. They are all about football and baseball. Louie is going to love these," Rory shared with another student. Just then, Louie walked into the classroom.

Rory ran over with the books. "Louie, look at this cool book about NFL football. Let's see if we can find the Miami Dolphins players."

Louie was ecstatic. He didn't even get around to unpacking his backpack that day.

After the kids settled in, Jen got their attention and asked them to join her over on the rug.

She said, "Boys and girls, what a fun way to start our day. You noticed the books I set out on the tables right away. Anybody find a book they might be interested in?"

One student said, "Mrs. McDonough, did a book order come in? Is that where all these books came from?"

"Actually," Jen replied, "these books have been in our class library all year long."

They look astonished. "Boys and girls, I thought because I knew what books we had in our classroom that you would too. But then, after talking to some of you, I realized that you really didn't know what great books we have all around us. Today, we are going to figure out together what books we have and how we want to put them in the library so we can all read them!"

One boy exclaimed, "Cool," and there were a lot of heads nodding.

"Okay, what kinds of books did we see on the tables?" Jen asked the class.

We heard shouts of dinosaur books, football, and books about penguins.

"Great," she said. "What else do you notice about the books?"

Margo raised her hand. "Things, real things, like things we can learn about."

"You got it. These books are information books. Does anyone know the special name we use for books that give us information?"

"Nonfiction!" the class yelled in unison.

Jen wrote "Nonfiction Information Books" at the top of the chart paper and listed topics the kids had shared with her.

"We're going to start reading our nonfiction books and figuring out how to put them in our library so we can really use them to explore questions and learn about new topics."

Jen explained to them how they now needed to break into small groups and look through all of the nonfiction information books in the classroom.

"First, we just want to look and see what books we have that you might be interested in reading," Jen said.

"Then, we need to start thinking about how we want to put the books together so that we can place them in bins and be able to find books from our library more easily."

Jen divided the kids into groups of three and gave each group a pile of nonfiction books to browse through. She gave them about five minutes to look through and discuss with their friends the books they had in front of them.

Jen then stopped the class and said, "Now we need to think about putting our books into groups."

She showed them a pile of books she had. Out of the seven books, two were about dinosaurs, one was about dolphins, one was about whales, one was about fish, one was about starfish, and one was about dogs.

"Hmm." Jen held up the books so they could see them. "I see that both of these books are about dinosaurs so I am going to start a dinosaur pile. These books are all about animals that live in the water, so I am going to put them in a pile. I guess this dog book can be on its own for now.

"Did you see how I looked at my books and tried to put them into groups if they had something in common? Now I want you to try the same thing with the books you have in front of you. See if you can say, 'These books are all about _____, after you put the books in piles.'"

Jen helps the students sort the nonfiction titles from the class-room library.

A group of first graders decides how to sort their books by topic.

Katie and Katrina decide which topics to use to sort their books.

Jen gave the kids another few minutes to try to group their books. Once the room was quiet again, she had the children share their groups of books with the rest of the class, using the prompt, "These books are all about _____."

This is when the groups started to make connections. When one group said, "These books are all about dinosaurs," Jen helped the class check to see whether any other groups had dinosaur books, and then they added their books to the pile of dinosaur books.

Jen then asked kids to take a pile of books with a partner, put the group of books into a plastic shoebox bin, and design a label for the front of the bin to tell others what the books were about.

When most of the books were in bins, we looked at the books that didn't seem to fit in any of the sorted bins. The class voted and decided to put them in a big basket that simply said "Nonfiction." Then after some thinking, the kids put the bins up in the front shelf of the classroom for the nonfiction study.

For books like the Magic School Bus series, which are written about different topics, the kids decided whether they wanted to break them up into different topics or keep the series in their own bins. They decided that it would be better to break them up if there was a bin, so the book on dinosaurs went into the dinosaur bin. However, if there were books left over that didn't have a place to go, they would keep those together in a Magic School Bus bin.

A couple of days later, Jen wanted to see whether all of their work had made it easier to identify the nonfiction books. She approached Louie as he walked in one morning.

"Hey, Louie. Good morning. How is your snail?" she asked.

"Great, Mrs. McDonough. I let him go because I thought he would probably be happier in the grass and the dirt than in a shoebox."

Letting the students organize and label the bins gives them a sense of ownership over the classroom library.

Ned and Katherine create a label for the "Weather" nonfiction book bin.

Lily labels the "Wonder" book bin.

The new and improved nonfiction section of Jen's classroom library

"Did you ever figure out what those snails like to eat?" she asked.

"Sure, while we were looking at all of our books the other day, we found a book about snails and put it in the animals bin. Then I put it in my book bag for reading workshop so I could find out. Snails are so cool, did you know . . . ," and the long list of facts about snails began.

Jen's Reflection

The categories the kids created were dinosaurs, earth and water, sports, rocks, plants, places, ocean and ocean animals, and spiders and bugs.

The classroom library books are sorted by topic.

Because I had already organized the books into bins, for the most part I made sure that the piles of books I gave to the children had a pattern that they could see quite easily: two or three dinosaur books for them to connect, a few books about ocean animals, and so on. If I had spread them out too much, it would have been harder for the children to see the patterns so quickly and easily at this point. After all of the books had been reorganized by the students this time, I handed out empty plastic shoebox bins and strips of white copy paper. I asked the groups to come up with a title for the bin, using the prompt, "What are the books in this bin mostly about?" and then I asked them to draw a picture to go with the title to give their friends picture and word clues. I insisted that "When in sight, spell it right," and asked them to use the titles and text of the books to correctly spell the titles on the bins. Here are the steps for sorting nonfiction books, based on a presentation given by my graduate reading professor, Dr. Jill Jones (2006):

1. Grab all the nonfiction bins you have in your classroom.

2. Put the books into seven different piles (three kids per pile). Mix the nonfiction books up a bit while leaving a few together so the kids start to see a pattern of topics or authors.

    (At this point, the kids will get excited about looking at the books in their piles, so give them time for browsing and sorting. This is when they discover what amazing nonfiction books are in our classrooms.)

3. Let the kids sort their books in the small groups by topic, author, series, and so on.

4. Ask the whole group whether anyone has any dinosaur books. Bug books? Magic School Bus books?

5. Ask kids to bring books that follow a topic and put them in one pile together.

6. Keep going until most of the books are in piles that can be binned and labeled.

7. Reassign kids to piles of books to put in the bin and create a label for the bin. (Cut strips of white paper or label stickers to give to the kids to write a title for the bin and maybe draw a picture to go with it.)

8. Have the kids put the bins in a special place in the classroom and feature the nonfiction books.

9. Books don't fit a pattern? Have the kids decide what to do with them. Give them ownership to decide.

This is guaranteed to get the kids excited about nonfiction books again.

After sorting the nonfiction books, Jen began a discussion with her students about the differences between nonfiction and fiction texts. She wrote her students' thinking on a chart.

The children helped develop this chart as they discussed the differences between fiction and nonfiction.

2. Exploring Nonfiction Books: Structures and Features

If you want to be a writer, you must do two things above all others: read a lot and write a lot . . . reading is the creative center of a writer's life . . . you cannot hope to sweep someone else away by the force of your writing until it has been done to you.

~ Stephen King

Before I begin a day of writing, I always start by sitting in my writing chair, feet up, a cup of coffee in my hand, and I read first. If I'm working on poetry, I read poetry. If I'm writing a professional book, I read professional books. Why? Because reading inspires me, gives me courage, and teaches me about craft.

A big reason Jen's students were so successful with writing nonfiction was that we simultaneously implemented aspects of question asking and wonderment in reading workshop. As we explored nonfiction in writing, we also explored nonfiction in reading. This allowed for strong, cohesive reading and writing connections. Therefore, our goals for this work included an introduction to the elements of reading nonfiction as we were simultaneously introducing the use of those same elements as writers. First, we wanted to demonstrate a nonfiction book's features and craft that students could then use in their own nonfiction books. Second, we wanted them to learn to be able to answer and to infer from books if their questions weren't explicitly answered in the text.

Resource Materials

✓ An assortment of nonfiction books with a variety of features. We used: *What Is Water?* by Robin Nelson, *What Makes a Magnet?* by Franklyn M. Branley, *What Do Authors Do?* by Eileen Christelow, *Why Do Volcanoes Blow Their Tops? Questions and Answers About Volcanoes and Earthquakes* by Melvin A. Berger, and *Apples* and *The Pumpkin Book* by Gail Gibbons.

✓ Blank chart

We wanted to discuss with young writers how writers' wonders and questions are explored in books, the different ways nonfiction books explore questions, and to begin to notice various features in informational nonfiction texts.

Jen gathered the children together and placed a basket of books on her lap. She wanted to share a variety of nonfiction with the children to introduce them to the genre.

"Today, I have a basket of books on my lap, and they are all similar," Jen said. "They are what I call nonfiction books. They all give us the information in different ways. Here are a few of these kinds of books."

Jen held the book up for the class to see and showed them the title. "This book is called *What Is Water?* The question is the title, and the entire book is an answer to the question. The author researched the question by looking in books, in magazines, and maybe on the Internet to find the answer, just like we researched your questions during Friday pondering time.

"Here are three other nonfiction books that do the same thing: *What Makes the Wind? What Do Authors Do?* and *What Makes a Magnet?* The information in these books comes from research like the way we answered many of your questions—from books, magazines, the Internet, and our brains. Here's the chart we made.

"Another type of nonfiction book includes lot of different questions and answers. For example, *Why Do Volcanoes Blow Their Tops? Questions and Answers About Volcanoes and Earthquakes.* The whole book has a bunch of questions and answers all about volcanoes and earthquakes." Jen held the book up and showed them all the questions. "Look at how many questions there are in this book.

"Why do volcanoes blow their tops? How hot is it inside the earth?"

Students oohed and ahed. John said, "Cool" when he saw the picture of the lava flowing down the volcano.

"There is also another type of nonfiction book," Jen continued.

Jen picked up *The Pumpkin Book* by Gail Gibbons and held it up for the class. "I know you know this book already because we read it at Halloween. It's about a big topic—pumpkins."

She then flipped through. "I'm also noticing that this book has different sections, like diagrams and a how-to section, and it's all about the big topic—pumpkins. For example, here's a section with a diagram, and here's a how-to section.

"And here's a book entitled *Apples*, which is an 'all-about book,' and it has a table of contents and chapters with different ideas in it, plus it's a big book.

"Writers, now you are going to try to see what kind of nonfiction books we have in the classroom," said Jen. "I'm going to give you and your partner a nonfiction book. Will you investigate together and see what kind of nonfiction in that book it is? Is your book like *What Is Water?* in that it asks one question and then explores the answer in the rest of the book? Or is it more like *Why Do Volcanoes Blow Their Tops? Questions and Answers About Volcanoes* in that there are many questions and answers in the book? Or is it like the third kind of book, *The Pumpkin Book,* where the book is all about one topic, but it has sections? Or maybe is it an all-about book with a table of contents and chapters?

"See what else you notice about your book. Does your book have photographs or pictures? Does it have diagrams (drawings with words)? Does it have a table of contents in the beginning of the book?"

We listened in on the kids as they investigated their books. After a few minutes with their partners, Jen conferred with them to find out what they noticed.

Griffin noticed that there were many questions in his book. Margo observed that the book had words in the back. Jen said, "Do you know what those words are called, Margo?"

Margo shook her head no.

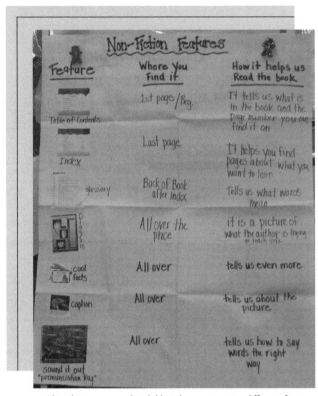

This chart grew as the children began to notice different features of the nonfiction books they were reading.

"That's called a glossary, and I'm glad you noticed it. Maybe you'll help me teach the other kids when we come back to the rug for sharing."

Noelle noticed that her nonfiction book repeated the word "why" throughout. Andres said to Jen, "My book has chapters in it!"

Jen invited the children back to the rug to discuss what they noticed about the nonfiction books. Jen wrote down their noticing on a chart:

What We Notice About Nonfiction Books

Nonfiction books sometimes:

- Ask one question and answer the question in the book
- Ask a lot of questions on one topic and answer the questions
- Are all about one topic with sections
- Are all about one topic with chapters

Nonfiction Book Features

Features	Where You Find It	How It Helps Us Read the Book
• Table of contents	• First page/beginning	• It tells us what is in the book and the page numbers you can find it on
• Glossary	• Back of the book (usually before index)	• Tells us what words mean
• Index	• Last page	• It helps us find pages about what we want to learn
• Diagrams	• All over the place	• It is a picture of what the author is trying to teach us
• Cool facts	• All over the place	• Tell us even more
• Captions	• All over the place	• Tell us about the pictures
• Sound-it-out/ pronunciation key	• All over the place	• Tells us how to say words the right way

Jen's Reflection

To begin, you'll want to collect a variety of nonfiction books that have different structures and features (see book list at the end of this chapter). Then create a chart with the heading "What We Notice About Nonfiction Books." Let kids explore the books and tell you what they noticed. Because of the immersion we had done prior to and during the nonfiction unit, the kids were already familiar with some of the features, such as table of contents, chapters, index, and glossary.

3. Getting Started: Choosing Research Wonder Topics

The crucial distinction for me is not the difference between fact and fiction, but the distinction between fact and truth. Because facts can exist without human intelligence, but truth cannot.

~ *Toni Morrison*

Facts are data; truth is the sense we make of the data.

~ *Scott Russell Sanders*

I am an avid "clipper." I clip on planes, in the morning while I'm drinking my coffee, anywhere and anytime. I have a file thick with scraps taken from newspapers and magazines and labeled "ideas and inspirations." Every few months, I take my folder out and mull over the articles. The snippets I save are there to assimilate and to inspire my writing and my life. I read over Joan Didion's words from a commencement address, "I'm just telling you to live in it. Not just to endure it, not just to suf-

Resource Materials

✓ Wonder boxes with children's wonders written on index cards

✓ Blank chart

✓ *The Pumpkin Book* by Gail Gibbons

✓ Topic planning sheet (*see Appendix*)

fer it, not just to pass through it, but to live in it" (Donadio 2005). Pieces of her commencement speech have made it into a keynote I once gave. After the poet Yehuda Amichai died, they found scraps—notes and jottings—saved in a box. One jotting encapsulates for me what it means to teach: "We do not wish to see the forest/We wish to see the trees, the tree./The child, not the human race" (Wieseltier 2004).

In teaching nonfiction research writing, we don't want children copying facts out of a book and calling it nonfiction. We want students to feel that a question they are exploring is personal and interesting enough to assimilate their explorations into their thinking and their writing.

Figure 3.1

Julia's research wonder, with the drawing of an eye indicating a research wonder

Figure 3.2

Nicole's research wonder

For this reason, we first asked the children in Jen's class to look through the questions in their wonder boxes and to pull out their research wonder index cards. They had written an amazing variety of research questions from their nonfiction reading and from their own experiences (see Figures 3.1 and 3.2).

Then we asked them to put all those wonders in a pile that were about something in the natural world. We noticed that researching and writing about the natural world was easier for them to start with and often made for more creative nonfiction pieces.

The children were ready to start selecting their topics for their nonfiction pieces based on their research wonders, and we created a mini-lesson for the next day.

"There are two steps that writers take when they want to write a nonfiction book. Let me remind you of what they are," Jen said, as she pointed to the chart paper and began to write and explain.

"First, you need to find a topic you have questions or wonders about and that you're really interested in finding out about, but you must also know a little something about this topic.

"The second step is that it really helps if, to start, you choose a topic from nature, like the ocean or stars, or a living thing, because those kinds of things are much easier to research and write about."

Jen held up *The Pumpkin Book* by Gail Gibbons and told the kids that Gibbons had chosen pumpkins as her topic. They discussed that, as a writer, Gibbons had a big decision to make before she started writing *The Pumpkin Book*. Did she know enough about pumpkins to write an entire book about them? Was she really interested in exploring more about pumpkins? And did she have questions or wonders about pumpkins that she wanted to research?

"Today, writers, I'd like you to think about the research wonders you chose from your wonder boxes and to ask yourselves: 'Could I write a whole book about it?' 'Is my topic big enough that I could write a whole book about it?'

"First, we're going to write a book together as a class and try out the two steps. The first step is deciding on a topic from nature that we know a lot about but have some wonders about."

The class brainstormed several topics, including the banyan tree in the schoolyard, afternoon thunderstorms, and the hermit crabs in the classroom. They decided on the hermit crabs since they keep them as pets, and the children know a lot about them from their daily interactions with them.

Jen said, "The second step is to decide if we know enough about the hermit crabs and if you have any wonders about them."

She turned to the chart and pointed to each step as she recited them to the class:

1. Think of a topic you know a lot about but still have some questions or wonders you want answered.

2. Choose a topic from nature, or a living thing.

"Every time you're ready to start a new nonfiction book with a different topic, use this chart to help remind you of the steps you need to take," said Jen. "This is really important to do because otherwise you could choose a topic that you don't know enough about. If that happens, you'll probably get stuck halfway through without enough information to complete your book. And we want a lot of information in our books, so they're interesting to read."

Then Jen sent the children back to their seats to read over their research wonders from their wonder boxes and asked them to select one of their research questions that might be a possible topic for their nonfiction books. Jen reminded them to use the steps on the chart.

Sam placed one of his research wonder index cards in front of him and was staring at it when Jen walked over to ask him about his topic. Sam said, "My wonder is, 'How to make snow?'"

Jen said, "So, what do you think your big topic for your nonfiction book might be?"

Sam hesitantly said, "Snow?"

Figure 3.3

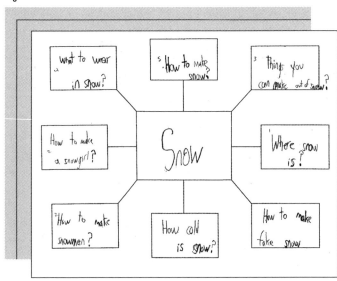

Sam planned his topic, snow, on an earlier version of a planning sheet.

"That's right. Do you know something about snow but still have some questions about it?"

Sam's face brightened, "I know a lot about snow, but I want to know how it's made."

Jen asked him to go get a planning sheet and to write down his questions about snow to see whether he wanted to keep this as a topic for his nonfiction book (see Figure 3.3).

Jen's Reflection

When you are conferring with kids as they brainstorm topics, encourage them to talk it out. Listen for whether they know enough about the topic and whether they have enough questions. You can usually tell if they aren't passionate about their topics, and then you can guide them in thinking about a topic they're really interested in exploring. For children who seem stuck, I send them over to the observation window to look outside and reread the class observation journal. I encourage them to reread their wonders in their wonder boxes.

We revised the planning sheet so that now it is divided into two sections. On the left side, on the top, we have "What I Know About My Topic," and on the right side, we have "What I Wonder About My Topic" (see Appendix).

4. Nonfiction Writing: Trying On Topics

You don't write because you want to say something,
you write because you've got something to say.

~ F. Scott Fitzgerald

In *The Revision Toolbox: Teaching Strategies That Work* (Heard 2002), I write about how, as a teenager, I used to go to the local five-and-ten store to try on sunglasses:

Resource Materials

✓ Topic planning sheet
   (*see Appendix*)

I owned at least a half-dozen pairs mostly because I thought sunglasses were cool, and partly because each new pair changed my perspective on the world: the yellow lenses always made the world seem oppressive and murky like I was swimming in a dirty river; the blue lenses created a rather disturbing cold world . . . ; and the rose-colored glasses made the world seem cheery and much warmer—especially in winter. (74)

Similarly, when I begin writing I try on different topics or different approaches to a topic as if I'm looking at it with different-colored lenses. Most of the time I just know that a topic doesn't feel right because it's difficult to write, and I'm not eager to work on it. But sometimes I don't know that a topic is wrong until I'm well into writing.

Jen gathered the children together to begin the mini-lesson on choosing the right topic.

"Today, I want you to watch closely as we walk through the steps authors take after they have picked a topic and before they even begin to write their books," Jen told the class. "Authors try on topics. They hold it up and say, 'Will the topic fit me? Do I like it?' In other words, after they decide on a topic, then they ask, 'Do I know enough about it to write a whole book? Do I have more questions about it? Is it a topic I'm really interested in? Are there any books or materials in the classroom about the topic?'

"Watch me closely as I think about possible topics that might work for me. Hmm. Let's see. I am going to think about things that I have questions about."

Jen showed the kids that she was thinking carefully, channeling all of her mental energy into discovering topics that might work.

"Umm. First, I'll try on the topic 'geckos' to see whether it fits and whether I know a lot about it," she told them. "Let's see. I've seen a gecko before, and my cousin had one. I know that a gecko is a reptile, and it doesn't have fur. Hmm. That's all I really know about them. I might be able to write a whole book about geckos, but I'm not sure if I really want to.

"One question I have about geckos is, 'Do geckos change colors?' But if I just answer this one question in my book, it won't be enough for a whole book. Instead my topic could be 'All About Geckos.' I might be able to write a whole book about that.

"You have to decide whether the question you asked in your research wonder is big enough and whether you can write a whole nonfiction book about it."

She made it obvious that she knows very little and cares very little about this topic.

"Hmm. I also know about grass. I step on grass all the time. I wonder what makes grass the color green. I could research this, but I don't think I'm interested in researching grass. What else? Oh! Hermit crabs are a great choice because we have those as class pets, and we already discovered that we know a lot about them. I still have questions about hermit crabs, and they are a living thing."

Jen held up the sheet of planning paper. "I know a lot about this topic. This one might fit me just right. I tried on the topic first just like a pair of glasses with different lenses and found that hermit crabs fit. We've already discovered that we know a lot about them, yet I still have some questions that I can research and find the answers to."

Jen pulled out a planning sheet or "thinking paper" divided into two columns: "What We Know About Hermit Crabs" and "Questions We Have About Hermit Crabs."

What We Know About Hermit Crabs

1. Hermit crabs drink by dipping their claws in water then lifting out drops of water to their gills and mouth.

2. Hermit crabs love to climb.

3. Hermit crabs are nocturnal. They move around a lot more at night than during the day.

"We know quite a bit already about hermit crabs. And now, what are some of your questions about hermit crabs?" Hands waved frantically in the air as students waited to be called on.

Questions We Have About Hermit Crabs

1. What do we feed them?

2. Do they jump off the side of their pool?

3. Are they afraid of dogs?

4. Do they like fresh water or salt water?

5. Are they afraid of fish?

6. How big do they get?

7. Why do they pinch?

8. Is Jerry afraid of Tom? (The hermit crabs are named Tom and Jerry.)

"Wow! We really do know enough about hermit crabs, and we have enough questions to fill a whole book. Plus, we have a few books in our classroom library about hermit crabs to help us answer questions. The next step is to take our planning sheet paper and decide on the sections of our book about hermit crabs. This will help us know what we still have to research about hermit crabs." At this point, Jen and I let the kids talk among themselves and decide on the topics of the hermit crab chapters.

After a few minutes, Jen asked that they turn their attention back to her. "Great job, writers. So now we know that there are two steps to starting a new nonfiction book.

"So, writers, today as you think about your topics for your nonfiction pieces, I want you to do what authors do and try on a few topics first. Remember, you're trying to figure out two things: one, if you feel that you know enough—and care enough—about your topic to write a whole book, and two, if you still have some unanswered questions that you can research to fill in the sections of your book. Remember to focus on living things or things from nature. Before you go back to your seats to work, I'd like you to turn and talk to your writing partner about your ideas. Partners, make sure that your partners' ideas follows all the steps that we talked about."

As the children shared, we listened in. Jen and I conferred quickly to guide them in making choices about the natural world and topics that would be manageable to research and write about.

Jen then said, "Writers, finish your sentences and then put your eyes on me. I heard Sam tell his partner that he was writing about snow because he goes to Boston where it snows a lot. He said he already knew something about snow but had some questions about it too. And Joseph is going to write about rocks because he collects rocks. He knows a lot about them but still has some questions about rocks, such as where different rocks come from. Today, I'm going to have you just think about what you already know about your topic. And then after a few minutes, I'm going to ask you what questions you still have."

Jen held up the topic planning sheet (see Appendix). Jen sent the kids back to write with a planning sheet to "try out" their topics. We conferred with the kids about their topics and wrote down their topics so that we could go to the class and school libraries to see how we could support them in their research. Jen and I had quick conferences with every child to make sure they knew enough about the topic and had some interesting questions they could research. A few children who struggled with finding a topic were directed to their wonder boxes to reread their questions.

After a conference, most kids began to write down what they knew about their topics and then started planning their ideas and creating sections of information they were going to teach their readers. We tried to steer them toward topics in the natural world.

John had chosen one of his research questions: "I wonder where plastic comes from?" Jen knelt down next to his desk for a conference and asked how he was doing. While John knew a few things about plastic, he really only had one question about plastic: "How is plastic made?" As Jen encouraged him to talk about his topic, she noticed that he didn't seem to be that engaged or passionate about it, other than finding out how plastic is made.

Jen said, "Remember we talked in our mini-lesson about choosing a topic from something in nature? Well, plastic is not so much in nature, and as I listened to you talk about it, you didn't seem to have too much to say about plastic, and did you notice that you only had one question about it? Usually, if I can't talk about a topic, it's hard to write about it. One thing that has helped me as a writer is to think about a topic in nature like we talked about in class today. It seems like topics in nature are easier to write more about. Do you have any other ideas, John, about something in nature?"

John said, "I'm wondering about who made seeds."

Jen asked, "That sounds interesting. What were you thinking the topic for your book might be?"

John said, "I guess, seeds."

Jen said, "What do you already know about seeds, and what questions do you have about seeds? Maybe you can use the planning sheet to try on your seed topic and see whether that fits."

John seemed excited to pursue another topic.

Jen's Reflection

Georgia and I noticed that kids seemed more passionate about topics and their voices emerged when topics were about the natural world. They were more able to sustain their exploration and writing of topics. Maybe that's because children observe the natural world every day, maybe that's because kids have so many questions about how the world works, or maybe that's because kids perceive the world with magical eyes and are awed by its mystery and beauty. Whatever the reason, we noticed that the true voices of kids emerged when we guided them toward nature topics. In previous years, kids had chosen topics such as football, clarinet, and gymnastics. These topics seemed fine for "how-to" books, but for exploring and writing nonfiction books of wonder, the kids' excitement and passion stalled after the initial topic choice. As kids become more experienced in exploring and writing individual topics, then they can begin to choose topics that are more difficult to research and write about.

Create a planning sheet (see Appendix) to help guide the students toward realizing whether they know enough about their topic and what questions they have. This step will save kids from abandoning topics after investing a lot of time and energy in exploring them.

Choosing Topics

We learned that the topics children chose to write about made a tremendous difference in the children's ability to sustain their nonfiction writing for more than one day. We learned the importance of guiding children in selecting topics that they could stick with and discover more information about.

For example, Lily had chosen to write about her best friend, Charlotte, and after spending a few days writing, and even after interviewing Charlotte, Lily stopped writing and told Jen she was stuck and couldn't think of anything else to write about. As Lily looked around the class, her classmates were immersed in writing and reading about their topics, and she began to walk around the classroom chatting to her friends. When Jen noticed what she was doing, she sat down with Lily and explained how she could start another piece on a different topic if there was nothing more to write about. Lily reread her wonder cards and decided that she was interested in learning more about bees and had many questions about them. Jen redirected her to begin another piece. Jen even led Lily over to the discovery table where someone had brought in a real honeycomb with honey inside a jar.

What we learned from Lily and from other children who chose to write about topics that were either personal and more suited to narrative or for which there were no materials in the classroom was to gently redirect them to other topics that they could sustain for more than a day or two.

During the topic selection days, we gave a quick read of all the children's topics. If someone had chosen a topic that we thought they might not be able to sustain, we made sure to have a conference immediately, wonder box in hand, to talk about their topic selection and help guide them in another direction.

5. Nonfiction Writing: Creating a Table of Contents

[Writing] . . . is a piece of architecture. . . . It's a building —
it has to have walls and floors and the bathrooms have to work.

~ John Irving

> ### Resource Materials
>
> ✓ Children's filled-out topic planning sheet
>
> ✓ Table of contents paper (*see Appendix*)
>
> ✓ Nonfiction books with tables of contents

When I begin writing a book, I first make a blueprint of possible ideas that help organize my thoughts. The blueprints vary according to the kind of book I'm writing. For *Creatures of the Earth, Sea, and Sky: Animal Poems*, I used the back pages of my notebook to make a table of contents to outline the kinds of animals and insects I wanted to write about. Many of my ideas in the table of contents never made it into the book. Planning the table of contents was part of my thinking process and is not a checklist of writing that I have to do.

Jen gave a mini-lesson to her students on creating a table of contents as an organizing tool.

"Writers, all of you have come up with a topic for your nonfiction books, have done a little research on your information, and are getting ready to start your table of contents page.

"Today I want to show you that the sections listed in your table of contents need to be big and stuffed full of information. We don't want our sections to have just one fact each, because that would make the chapters too small," Jen told them. "If we were reading a book on ladybugs, and we opened the book to the table of contents page and read 'Ladybugs Have Black Spots,' that doesn't explain much about what ladybugs look like. It would be better to have a bigger chapter, like 'The Many Different Parts of a Ladybug.'

"Okay, writers. Let's look at the planning page for our hermit crab book. I'm going to read aloud the sections we were thinking about":

- What do you feed hermit crabs?
- The hermit crab likes to climb.
- Do they like fresh water or salt water?
- Hermit crabs live in shells.
- What are the parts of a hermit crab's body?
- Hermit crabs make great pets!
- How big do they get?

Jen slipped in some examples ahead of time that were too small, such as "The hermit crab likes to climb" and "Hermit crabs live in shells." She said, "Will you turn to your writing partner and discuss whether you think any of my section topics are too small to write an entire chapter on?" She listened in on the children's conversations and then asked for their attention again. Together, Jen and the class deleted the smaller topics, like "The hermit crab likes to climb" and "Hermit crabs live in shells," from the table of contents using the children's suggestions.

"Readers of nonfiction books turn to a table of contents to find information in a book. Watch closely as I write down on this chart what we know about the table of contents."

Jen took a few moments to leaf through some books she had collected earlier.

"A table of contents is always in the front of the book. It's in the front so I can skim through what I'm going to read first, and if I'm looking for specific information, I can glance through and see where I can find it.

"So, writers, today I'd like you to take the table of contents paper (see Appendix) and write down the big chapters that you'll have in your nonfiction book. Remember most of you already have a planning page. You can reread your sections to make sure they're big enough for separate chapters."

After the kids walked to their seats to write, I conferred with Sam, who had his planning sheet next to his blank table of contents page. He reread his planning sheet. I asked him, "What are you thinking Sam?"

He replied, "I'm trying to decide which one should go first."

"Which one are you thinking should go first?"

Sam said, "I think the biggest one, 'Where is snow?' should go first."

"That makes sense," I told him. "Sam, are there any sections on your planning sheet that you think are too small for a chapter?"

"Hmm," Sam said. "I think, 'How to make fake snow?' doesn't really go with the others, so I'm not going to write that one."

"Okay, Sam," I said. "I like the way you're rereading and thinking through your table of contents page."

Jen's Reflection

Creating a special table of contents page (see Appendix) to help children plan out their chapters before they write is an essential organization tool before writing begins. It's a prewriting tool, really, to help guide young writers in seeing what information they still need to gather. Although not all nonfiction books have a table of contents, it was a convention that we thought was important to introduce. (Our page was inspired by Lucy Calkins's work in The Units of Study for Primary Writing *[2003].)*

Most children will be writing two tables of contents: the initial table of contents to help them focus and organize their thinking and the second revised table of contents after they spend time writing, researching, and adding to their writing.

For example, Katie's book was about horses, and after a week of researching and writing, she went back and revised her table of contents to reflect her new ideas (see Figure 3.4).

Figure 3.4

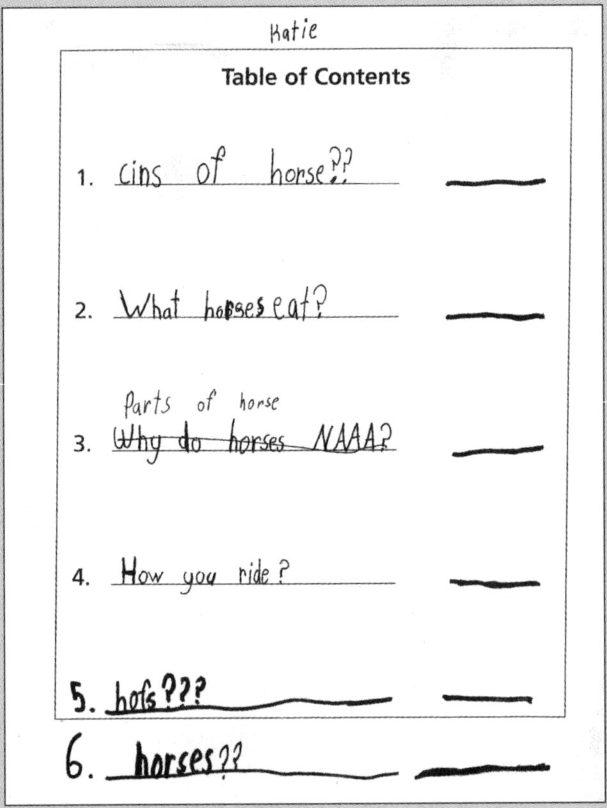

Katie

Table of Contents

1. cins of horse???
2. What horses eat?
3. ~~Why do horses NAAA?~~ Parts of horse
4. How you ride?
5. hofs???
6. horses??

Katie's revised table of contents

6. Nonfiction Writing: Designing Chapters

Writing is thinking on paper.

~ *William Zinsser*

"Writers, on Tuesday we began writing our table of contents," Jen told the kids as they gathered on the rug. "You all have such great ideas, and I can't wait to read your writing. I know I'm going to learn so much!"

Jen wanted the kids to know how excited she was to read their work before they launched into creating chapters.

Resource Materials

✓ Children's completed table of contents planning page

✓ Chapter paper *(see Appendix)*

"I heard some of you refer to the sections of your table of contents as chapters, so today I'm going to talk to you about how to take one of the ideas from your table of contents and turn it into a chapter.

"Okay, so our class book is about hermit crabs, like the ones right in our classroom. Here is our table of contents." She held up the table of contents and read it to the class:

- What do hermit crabs eat and drink?

- Where do hermit crabs live?

- Why and how do they change their shells?

- What are the parts of a hermit crab's body?

"Now, all of the items on the table of contents are important, and I may want to turn them all into chapters eventually, but right now I want to pick just one and stick with it. I don't want to rush through the chapter so I can get to the next one.

"Earlier I decided to work on this chapter about hermit crabs." Jen held up a sheet of planning paper and said, "After I looked at my table of contents and selected the topic I wanted to work on, I wrote the title of my chapter on this special paper. I did a quick sketch, and then I did my writing."

She paused for a minute to let the class look at this example: "Where Do Hermit Crabs Live?"

"Think of your chapter title as your 'big idea.' Every sentence should be connected to your title in some way. Let me read to you an example from my chapter, so you can see what I mean."

As she read a hermit crab chapter, she pointed out the important information she included, as well as the idea that each sentence should connect to the big idea: "Hermit crabs need to live on land but need water to drink and keep them moist. They usually live on rocks." (If you feel that your kids aren't completely clear on this point, you could give them an example of something you wanted to include but didn't because you ultimately decided it didn't connect to your big idea and left it out.)

"So, do you see how I selected a topic from my table of contents, got my paper, jotted down my title, and then wrote?

"Before you go off to write today, I want you to select your topic for your first chapter," Jen said. The kids were sitting on their folders, so they were able to get to their table of contents with as little interruption as possible.

Jen said, "After you have selected your topic I will give you time to talk to your partner about it. Then you will be ready to go off and begin your first chapter."

Jen gave the kids a few minutes to discuss their topics with their writing partners and asked for their attention once more. "Writers, as you work on your topics and add more chapters to your books, I want you to follow the steps I showed you. Really take your time to develop each chapter. If it is important enough to be on your table of contents, it is important enough to take your time to write about it. If you find that you don't have enough information, then you can do some research in books or on the computer."

Jen's Reflection

Creating a special chapter page (see Appendix) to help children plan out their chapters before they write is an organization tool that helps them organize their thoughts and focus their ideas.

Nonfiction Writing Shares

After a writer reads her or his piece in the author's chair at the end of the writing workshop, we ask the class to tell the author whether they have any wonders about the piece. When Gio shared the beginning of his piece about geckos, one question was, "I wonder are there different kinds of geckos?" Since Gio is an expert on geckos and has several different kinds, he started to explain. Jen stopped him and said, "Why don't you take a wonder card, write that question down, and put it in your folder to write about tomorrow during writing workshop." Next to the paper choices, we have index cards so that children can write down the information or questions during the share that authors might want to add to their pieces.

7. Exploring and Researching Questions

The possession of knowledge does not kill the sense of wonder and mystery.
There is always more mystery.

~ *Anaïs Nin*

The days spent sorting and trying on topics gave us time to gather the resources the kids needed to explore their questions through research. It was also enough time for the kids to decide whether the topic they had chosen was working, and if not, they had time to begin exploring alternatives.

We first enlisted the help of our amazing librarian. We had written down a list of the topics the kids were writing about

Resource Materials

✓ Nonfiction books on students' topics

✓ Computer

✓ Available adults *(optional)*

Andres observes a crystal for his nonfiction book.

and asked whether she could help gather some age-appropriate books for the children to look through. The list of topics included snow, dogs, rocks, bugs, crystals, turtles, apples, horses, and butterflies. She was happy to help, and we were able to pick up a pile of books to bring back to the classroom.

While the librarian was busy collecting books, we also browsed Web sites on topics writers had chosen and for which no books were available in the library. We found several kid-friendly sites, and we put them under the "favorites" section on the classroom computers.

Finally, we prepared a letter that would go home to the parents with space for the students to write down their questions about their topics that could be explored and answered at home (see page 127 in this chapter; also see Appendix).

Once we had all of these research venues in place, we invited any available adult in the school (or parent) to come and help. The day students researched was busy, exciting, and a little chaotic. Each child was researching and writing about a different topic and had different needs for resources. Having adult volunteers to guide kids in looking through books and to navigate the computer helped students feel successful. If adult volunteers are not available, research can still be accomplished with one teacher. It just takes more structure and patience.

We set up research stations around the classroom supervised by adults. On the reading rug, I sat next to a stack of books from the library on the topics the writers had chosen. Mrs. Meehan, the classroom assistant, sat at the computers. Mrs. Basil, the intermediate literacy coach, would rotate among the kids at their desks writing. Jen would help the children who were writing about something they had observed outside. Once we had the volunteers assigned and the stations set up, we gathered the children together for research day.

Jen explained, "Writers, you have all been working hard and writing down what you know about your topic. I know a lot of you still have some questions about your topics that you want to answer and write about in your books. When writers want to find answers to questions, they do something called research. I know we talked about this when you were writing down your wonders for your wonder boxes and in our wonder of the week pondering time. Remember what we talked about? That research is just like it sounds, you go out and search for an answer. We know that we can find answers to our questions in books, on the computer, by asking other people who might know the answer, and if possible, by looking at our topic with our own eyes to see what we notice about it. Today, we are going to try all of these things to find our answers. We've set up research stations around the room, and there will be an adult at each station who will help you explore the questions you have about your topic.

Georgia and students sit on the rug and read books on the same topic as their nonfiction writing pieces. They will then leave the books on the rug and go back to their writing spots to add to their pieces.

"One research station will be here on the carpet. We went to the library and found books about your topics, and some of the answers to your questions might be inside those books. Ms. Heard will be there to help you."

Jen continued, "Another station is at the computers. We found Web sites about your topics that might help you explore your questions, and Ms. Meehan will be there to help you if you have any trouble.

Emma researches questions to add to her nonfiction book.

Students research their topics on the computers.

"Mrs. Basil will help writers who will be writing about things they already know or who are waiting their turn at a research station.

"And I'll be outside helping those writers who need to do a little observational research on their topics."

We sent the kids back to their seats and asked them, first, to reread what they had written so far, and, second, to review the questions that they wanted to explore.

Jen asked, "Writers, who thinks they are ready to look in books to explore some of your questions?" Jen looked at the raised hands and sent five students to the reading rug, reminding the others that they would have a turn. She asked the same about the computer research station and the observation area outside the classroom. Children who had not been chosen to go to a research station in the room were asked to stay at their seats. Jen reminded them to keep writing about what they knew about their topics and then to add any questions they wanted to explore.

We noticed that as soon as the kids who were exploring their questions in books and on the computer found some of the answers they were looking

Louisa reads about her writing topic at the book research station.

for, they proceeded back to their seats to add new information to their books, thus clearing the way for others who were waiting a turn. Copying information from a book was not allowed. They knew beforehand that books could not leave the rug. After they explored their question, they returned to their seats to write down what they remembered, but not word for word. The same ruled applied to computer work.

Jen took a few kids outside so they could observe. An exciting part of the research happened outside.

Joseph wanted to see in what different places he could find rocks. Jack and Jamie studied leaves, and Nicole wrote about different types of flowers. As they stood outside, Jen approached Jamie and asked her what question she was trying to answer. She looked up at Jen and said, "I'm trying to figure out how leaves fall." Suddenly, the wind picked up and leaves started falling on our heads from the huge banyan tree. The other three kids noticed and started running around trying to catch them before they fell on the ground.

Nicole observes a flower and adds to her nonfiction book.

Jack observes a leaf to help him make a diagram for his "Leaves" expert book.

Jen said, "Jamie, quick, watch the leaves. What do you notice?"

Jamie said, "Oh, that's the wind's job. To make sure the leaves fall."

It was a poignant moment of observation, and Jen couldn't wait to go in and tell the others what had happened. Cheeks flushed with excitement, the kids ran back in to tell their fellow writers the story, and Jamie got right to work on an illustration of the leaves falling from the tree.

That night for homework the children put any remaining questions they had or couldn't find the answer to in the space provided on the parent letter. The children investigated their questions and brought the sheets back to school the next day.

As the kids continued to write their nonfiction books, Jen and I noticed that their writing was full of voice and that they used a variety of nonfiction structures and conventions.

Jen's Reflection

For teachers without adult support at school or from home, introduce one research station a day. On one day, pass out different-level books on topics, and invite all children to explore their questions in these books. Afterward, discuss what they have learned with a writing partner. After you collect the books, ask students to return to their seats to add what they've learned into their writing pieces.

For the computer research station, use your school's computer lab, and teach students how to search the Internet (safely) for information on their topics. Bookmark favorite Web sites before they begin, and make sure the computers don't have any technical glitches. Provide a guiding worksheet for them to write the answers to some of their questions as they find them on the computer. They can take the sheet back to the classroom to add to their writing pieces.

Take all of the children outside together. If their topic cannot be observed, then pair up students and have them help that author observe. Then have everyone go back inside to write.

We also enlisted the help of the school's wonderful science teacher, Mrs. Ruest, and invited her to be a guest speaker to answer any remaining questions. After she left, the students went back to their writing pieces to add what they had learned from "our expert."

Reading: What Do You Wonder About?

After the children chose their nonfiction topics, they read and glanced at the pictures in books about their topics during reading workshop. "What do you wonder?" was a question we encouraged them to ask, not just during writing workshop but also when they were reading about their topics during reading workshop. We created a "think" sheet to guide their thinking. In Figure 3.5, on the left-hand side are Nicole's wonders before reading her nonfiction book, and on the right-hand side are her answers on sticky notes after reading.

Figure 3.5

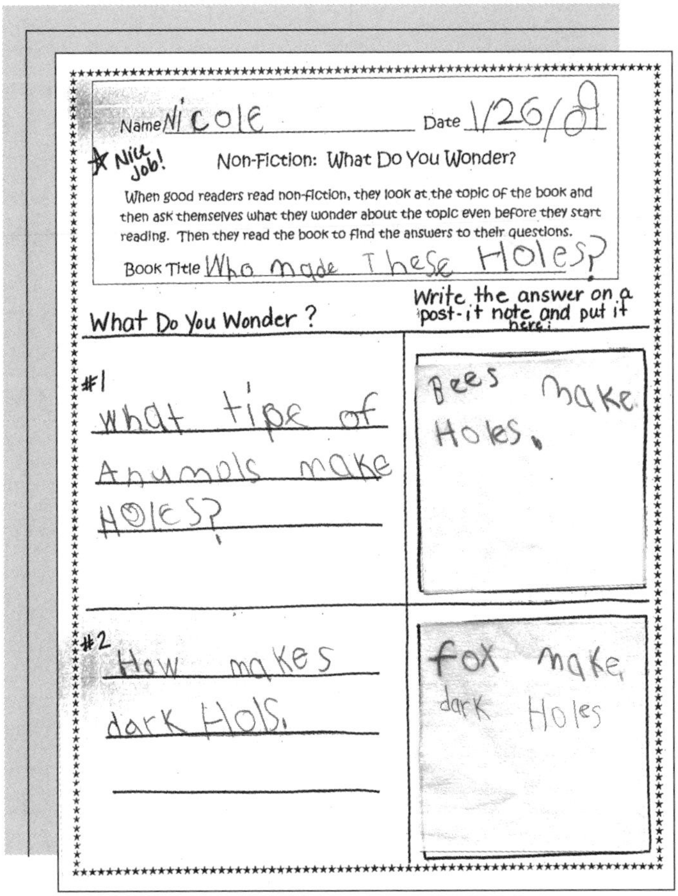

Name Nicole Date 1/26/09

Nice Job!

Non-Fiction: What Do You Wonder?

When good readers read non-fiction, they look at the topic of the book and then ask themselves what they wonder about the topic even before they start reading. Then they read the book to find the answers to their questions.

Book Title Who made These Holes?

What Do You Wonder? | Write the answer on a post-it note and put it here:

#1 what tipe of Anumols make HOlES? | Bees make Holes.

#2 How makes dark Hols. | fox make dark Holes

Nicole's "What do you wonder?" reading sheet

8. Exploring and Researching Questions: Inferring

There is creative reading as well as creative writing.

~ *Ralph Waldo Emerson*

Resource Materials

✓ Large chart and easel

✓ Nonfiction book for inferring

Some kids were reading nonfiction books and looking at Web sites on the computer and were not finding the information they needed to answer some of their questions. We discussed how kids were looking for the question and answer to appear exactly as they had written it down on their planning pages. Jen gave a mini-lesson the next day on *inferring*, modeling it with a book they all knew, entitled *Diving Deep* by Mark Strong. Jen reread the book, and the children were encouraged to ask questions about diving, which Jen wrote down on a chart: "How long can you stay underwater?" "How do people breathe underwater?" "Why do divers dive?" "What kind of food do some divers dive for?" "What do divers do with the treasure they find?"

Jen said, "We were able to find some of our answers in the book, like 'How do people breathe under water?'"

She read the table of contents, and when she read the chapter titled "Underwater Breathing," she told the kids that it said to turn to page 4.

Jen read aloud, "'Divers need equipment that lets them breathe under the water. This is called scuba equipment.' And now if I look closely at the photograph, I can see what the equipment looks like." She showed the photo to the children.

"Our question was answered in the book, so I'm going to write a big *B* next to it so we remember that the answer is in the book," she said. "But look at this question, 'What do divers do with the treasures they find?' Let's first look through the book and try to find an answer in the book. We've tried looking in the text for this answer, but we can't find it. We're going to have to come up with another way to answer this question.

"I'm going to show you how to use a reading strategy called *inferring*. Inferring means that you use thinking to understand something or to find the meaning. You won't always be able to find your exact question with the exact answer in the book when you're researching your topic," Jen told the kids as she picked up *Diving Deep* again. "So let's reread this question, 'What do divers do with the treasures they find?' Well, let me see if I can find the answer in the book."

Again, Jen skimmed through the book, wading in and out of sections where the answer might have been. Then she asked the kids if a possible answer was found in the text. They all agreed that, no, the answer wasn't in the book.

"I might first read the table of contents (if a book has one) to see if the word *treasure* is in there. I have to pay attention to the important words in my question, so I'll know what to look for. No, I don't see my question there or even the word *treasure*. Hmm. Next, I'll skim through the book and look closely at the pictures to see if I see any pictures of treasure. Hey, look! This chapter 'Shipwrecks' has a photograph of gold coins, which is treasure, isn't it? Here is the label, or the caption, that explains the picture, 'Sometimes divers find treasure!' but it doesn't say exactly what divers do with the treasure."

Jen said, "Okay, now let's try to infer the answer. It kind of means putting different bits of information together to get the answer. Think about what you know from your own experiences, and try to come up with a possible answer. Be sure to also use the picture in the books to help you."

She gave them a few minutes to think and asked them to turn to their partners and discuss whether they were able to infer an answer. We listened in.

Hunter said that he sees gold coins in the shipwreck chapter. He once heard about a group of people who found gold treasure and sold it for lots of money but also kept a few pieces for themselves. Hunter guessed that maybe that's what divers do with the treasure they find; they sell some and keep some. Daniela said that she's been to the Mel Fisher Treasure Museum in Key West, Florida, and they show the treasures like in a museum but they also keep some treasures for themselves.

Jen said, "See how you were able to answer the question from picture clues and your our own experiences? Kind of like we answered our heart wonders."

Jen then wrote an *I* next to the question, "What do divers do with the treasures they find?"

Jen said, "So, today, writers, those of you who haven't been able to find any answers to your questions in books or on the computer can infer to help answer your questions."

Here is a list of some of the strategies we use when we read and try to find answers to questions:

- Think about what we already know

- Think about our own experiences

- Reread

- Look closely at the photographs and illustrations

- Look in the table of contents

- Look in the index

- Look for important words in the table of contents and in picture captions

- Think about the question

Jen's Reflection

Kathy Collins's book Growing Readers *(2004) is an inspiration for all the primary teachers in our school. She explains many practical and useful strategies to guide kids in inferring information in nonfiction books.*

Nonfiction Book Clubs

Independent Reading—Children read their nonfiction books on their topics for about ten minutes or so.

Partner Reading—Children got into groups of four. Children had a turn to be the expert and share what they had learned so far about their topic. As the other children in the group listened, they wrote down one thing they learned on a sheet.

Share—We sat in a circle and each child picked one thing they learned from their book club group.

Reading Nonfiction: What Do You Expect to Learn?

Kathy Collins, author of the wonderful *Growing Readers*, discusses a mini-lesson about teaching kids to ask themselves, "What do I expect to learn?" before reading a nonfiction piece.

After this mini-lesson, Jen introduced a worksheet kids could use for identifying questions that could be found in the text and those that had to be inferred.

Name: _____ Date: _____

Book Title: _____

These are the questions I asked B (before), D (during), and A (after) reading my book:

After talking with my partner, I discovered that I could find some of the answers in the text (T) and some I had to infer (I). (Mark your sentences above with either a T or an I.)

9. Exploring and Researching Questions: Ask an Expert

If a child is to keep alive his inborn sense of wonder,
he needs the companionship of at least one adult who can share it,
rediscovering with him the joy, excitement and mystery of the world we live in.

~ Rachel Carson

Resource Materials

✓ Family letter
  (see Appendix)

✓ Experts from school
  community

When Jen's colleague Kristin visited her room one day, she looked at all the kids scattered around the room and said, "This feels different than my nonfiction writing workshop." Some of the kids were on the rug looking through books about their chosen topics, some were already researching on the computer, some were outside sketching leaves and grass and the banyan tree, and others were at their desks writing. They were completely immersed in their work. "How did you make this happen?" she asked.

Kristin hadn't started nonfiction and wonder work with her class yet, because we wanted to iron out the kinks before Jen presented it to her team. As Jen took Kristin around the room, she pointed out the kids' work and how our wonder work was affecting their writing. Jen remembered that Kristin had named her new baby "Banyan" and that one of Jen's kids happened to be writing an expert book on banyan trees.

"You could really help out Josh since you're an expert on banyan trees," she told her. "Would you help us?"

We gathered the kids together, but instead of a typical share session, we discussed the different ways we had learned to research answers to our questions.

"Another way to research your questions is to ask someone who's an expert on your topic," Jen said. "And we're lucky today because we have an expert on banyan trees right here with us. And Josh is going to ask Kristin a little bit about his topic, banyan trees. He wrote down some questions to ask her."

Kristin told them about naming her son "Banyan," and Josh started asking questions about banyan trees.

"Why do banyan trees have so many roots?" Josh asked. Kristin told him that the banyan's roots make the tree extra sturdy and grounded. Because of this, these trees have survived many hurricanes and strong winds when others haven't. Even if the trees are uprooted, she told the kids, the roots can reroot themselves right then and there.

Josh was impressed with Kristin's knowledge on his subject and asked whether he could please go back to his seat and add to his book.

The kids were so excited about conferring with experts that they all wanted to find experts on their own topics. We had drafted a letter for the kids to take home. We asked their parents to help them find an expert, or another research outlet, to find answers to their questions.

Dear Families,

Over the coming weeks, your child will be exploring questions and wonders about the world and how it works. Your child would like to explore the following question:

_____

One way we are teaching our young writers to research their questions is to interview other people to find out what they know about the topic. Please help your child answer his or her question by answering it yourself or calling on a friend or family member who may be more of an "expert" on the topic. Please help your child write and/or draw what he or she learns on the back of this sheet and return it tomorrow. They will be using this information to help write a nonfiction book based on their question.

Thanks for your help and support!

The letter was a great success. The kids arrived the next morning buzzing with "guess whats" and "you gotta hear this." Louie immediately consulted the class calendar for the day and announced the time when writing workshop would begin. Jen decided that she didn't want their enthusiasm to fade as the day progressed and rearranged the class schedule so the kids could get all this energy into their nonfiction books.

Noelle was excited to be the first person in the author's chair to share her information gathered from consulting an "expert"—her mother. Her question was, "How did they make the first seed?" Noelle wrote down her thoughts on a sheet Jen had created. She answered her question from what she thought and believed to be true. She then created a diagram of her thoughts after

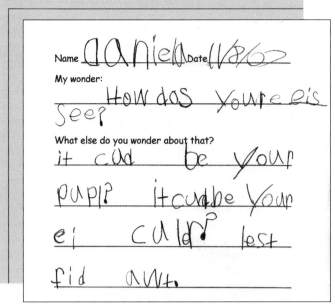

Name daniela Date 11/8/62

My wonder:

How dos youre eis see?

What else do you wonder about that?

it cud be your pupl? itcudbe your ei culd lest fid awt.

Daniela's think sheet on her topic, "How does your eye see?"

Figure 3.7

The eye sees and takes in information about the world around us. The light passes through the iris, pupil & lens and the image shows up in the retina upside down. The optic nerve serves as a messenger to the brain. The brain tells you what you see by flipping the image around.

Retina

Iris Pupil

lens

optic nerve

Daniela's mother shares her expertise on eyes.

doing a little reading about seeds that day. When Jen sent the letter home that night, Noelle and her mother discussed her question, and it became clear to Noelle that her mother also wondered how seeds grew. When her mother explained a seed's growth process Noelle wrote what she remembered after consulting her mom, the expert. She read her information to the class the next day.

Daniela also had a research wonder, "How does your eye see?" which she tried to answer by asking more questions (see Figure 3.6). When the letter went home that night, Daniela shared her question with an expert—her mother. She was an eye doctor who explained how eyes see in detail (see Figure 3.7).

There were many children who didn't have someone to ask at home, and when we conferred with them, we came up with experts at school or someone at another child's home who was an expert.

Jen brought out the chart they had created during their wonder of the week pondering time session, when the children learned how to research questions. She reminded the children about how authors go about gathering information for their nonfiction books. The chart read:

How We Explore Research Wonders

- Read and look in books
- See it on television
- Read and look in magazines
- Look on the Internet
- Use our hearts and brains

Jen reminded them that they had one more way to explore their questions. And a few of the kids responded in unison:

- Ask an expert

Jen's Reflection

If you have a lot of parent involvement in your school, then enlist the parents to help with the work. If you don't, enlist the help of teachers and other staff members who may have a specialty they can talk to the students about. Look around your community for people that could come in as guest speakers. Experts can be found in diverse places. I found our science teacher through the librarian, who gathered the books for us and happened to mention how knowledgeable this teacher was about nature. Ask around. You never know what interests and insights people have that they can share.

10. Nonfiction Writing: Leads/Beginnings

The most important sentence in a good book is the first one.

~ *Paul Horgan*

Jen and I discussed how, just as in picture books, authors of nonfiction books also want to capture the reader's attention from the first line.

Jen began the mini-lesson:

"Writers, I want to talk to you about something that writers do when they start books. They try to grab the reader's attention by making the very first sentence interesting so the reader will want to keep reading. I want to talk to you about three ways that writers do this.

"The first way you can begin your nonfiction writing is by asking a question. Questions grab the reader's attention, especially if it's an interesting question. Remember the book *Have You Seen Bugs?* by Joanne Oppenheim? That book begins with a question, 'Have you seen bugs?'

"Another way writers can capture the reader's attention is by stating a really interesting fact in the first sentence. We could start our hermit crab book with, 'There are 800 different kinds of hermit crabs!'

"Now, wouldn't that grab a reader's attention?

"And the third way writers can begin a nonfiction piece is by writing interesting sound words." Jen read from a volcano book that began, "RRRRuummmble! SSSSSSSrrra! Ker boom!"

One of the kids yelled out, "Onomatopoeia!"

"Yes," Jen said. "You're right, it is onomatopoeia.

"Today, I want you to get out your nonfiction pieces and reread your beginnings. Is it a beginning that will grab the reader? Will it make them want to read more? If not, get out your pencil and try another beginning—a question, an interesting fact, or a sound word."

As Jen and I walked around and conferred with students, we noticed that a lot of the kids began their pieces with questions. A few revised their beginnings, like Andrew who was writing about crabs. He changed his beginning from "I see crabs" to "Scratch, scratch, scratch, that's the sound of crab claws on the sand." And Tommy began one of his chapters, "Chomp, chomp. That's the sound of the tiger eating its prey!"

Jen's Reflection

Georgia and I noticed that most of the kids wanted to begin their pieces with a sound or a noise. We had to remind them that the sound had to make sense and feel true to the reader. Ryan was writing about crystals and wanted to begin his piece with a sound, but after a conference, he agreed that a sound wouldn't really make sense unless it were the sound of rocks being crushed.

During conferences, we reminded the writers that the start of each new chapter could have an interesting beginning as well.

---

11. Nonfiction Writing: Wow Words

One must be drenched in words, literally soaked in them.

~ *Hart Crane*

The children were beginning to draft their nonfiction books, and we noticed that some of the words they were using were vague and generalized: lizards were "big and small," crystals were "colorful," and dogs were "different kinds." Jen and I discussed how we could talk to the students about crafting words in nonfiction writing and about using vivid, descriptive, and, as Jen refers to them, "wow" words.

Resource Materials

✔ Wow word sheet
   (see Appendix)

✔ Nonfiction books with wonderful words

Jen began earlier in the day by reading aloud *Have You Seen Bugs?* by Joanne Oppenheim. Later on, during writing workshop, Jen reread the book and pointed out that the author could have described the bugs with boring words like *big*, *small*, or *colorful*. Instead, she used vivid words that described and gave us a picture in our minds of the bugs.

Jen said, "Listen to some of the words Joanne Oppenheim, the author, uses to describe the different kinds of bugs." Jen read:

> *Itty-bitty bugs/small as specks of sand. . . . Iridescent bugs/that shimmer in the light . . . winking, blinking bugs.*

"Did anybody hear any wow words?" Jen said. A few hands went up immediately as they shared some of the wow words.

"Let's try thinking of using really exact, descriptive words in our nonfiction book about our hermit crabs."

Jen walked over and took a hermit crab out of its cage. Some of the kids warned, "Be careful Mrs. McDonough, it will bite you!"

Jen sat down and said, "Let's write a chapter describing what the hermit crab looks like."

Jen wrote on a chart, "What a Hermit Crab Looks Like: The hermit crab has a shell. It is brown and small."

"I'm using boring words to describe the hermit crab: 'brown,' 'small,' 'has a shell.' I can do better than that. I'm going to show you the hermit crab close up, and let's think of wow words—descriptive words—that will really show what the hermit crab looks like."

Jen held the hermit crab and tiptoed carefully through the children as they gazed close-up at the hermit crab. "I hear such descriptions as, 'swirly,' 'bumpity,' 'spotted legs,' 'two-tiered eyes.'"

Jen wrote on the chart, "The hermit crab has a swirly, bumpity shell. It has spotted legs and two-tiered eyes."

"That's much better," she said. "What do you think, writers, about the words you're using?" The kids shout out words like "spectacular" and "wow."

Jen said, "When you return to your tables, I'd like you to take out your nonfiction books, reread the first page, circle one or two words that you think are boring, and think of wow words. Write the wow words above the boring words."

After the children settled into writing, we looked over their shoulders as they began. I noticed that some kids got to work right away. One boy had circled the words "they" and "are" and said to me, "What's a wow word for 'are'?" Jen and I quickly read over their shoulders and realized that we needed to have quick conferences to check in with the writers or move aside a table to have a group conference on the rug. The most difficult part of this craft/revision lesson was identifying which words to revise.

Alex was writing about dogs and had written on her first page, "Dogs do play games." When I conferred with her, I asked her what word she could replace with a wow word. She said, "games."

I asked, "What other words are you thinking of for 'games'?"

Alex said, 'Fetch' and 'gymnastics.'"

I responded, "So, how would you write your new words?"

Alex said, "Dogs play games like fetch and gymnastics."

"Alex, you've given us a real description of the games that dogs play. Great job."

When I conferred with Tommy, I noticed that he had changed his piece about tigers from "Some tigers are *white*. And some tigers are *striped*." To "Some tigers are *albino*. And some tigers have *black and orange stripes*."

Emma, who sat next to him, gave him the word "albino," and, although he thought of other words for "white," such as "paper" and "snow," he loved using this new word, "albino."

Gio, the expert on geckos, had written, "What kinds of geckos are there? Leopard geckos and lusistic geckos."

"Gio, what are lusistic geckos?" I asked.

He said, "It's a type of gecko. See, over here I made a poster of geckos."

Gio led me over to his poster displayed on the wall near the nonfiction books. The poster had real photographs of his geckos, and beneath one of them was the word "lusistic."

Figure 3.8

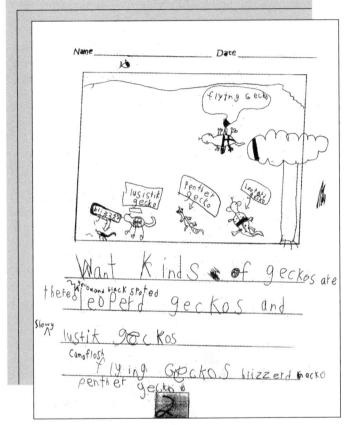

Gio's revised gecko piece using wow words

"I learned a new word today. Can I see your wow words?"

Gio had written, "Yellow and black spotted leopard geckos and snowy lusistic geckos" (see Figure 3.8).

As Jen and I reflected on this craft lesson, we talked about how the most difficult part of the revision process was identifying words to revise. A few of the kids weren't sure what words to choose, and Jen and I concurred that after the mini-lesson, it was essential to confer with students table by table to make sure that each child had chosen one word.

Jen's Reflection

I noticed that after this mini-lesson, kids became more aware of the words they were using. Not all writers revised their words that day, but during subsequent days, I would remind them in conferences about using detailed words. In conference with Harry a few days later, he had written, "Apples are different colors." And when I reminded him of using wow and detailed words, he added to his piece.

We also gave out a wow word brainstorming sheet so that writers could try revising words in their piece. Katie's sheet is shown in Figure 3.9.

Figure 3.9

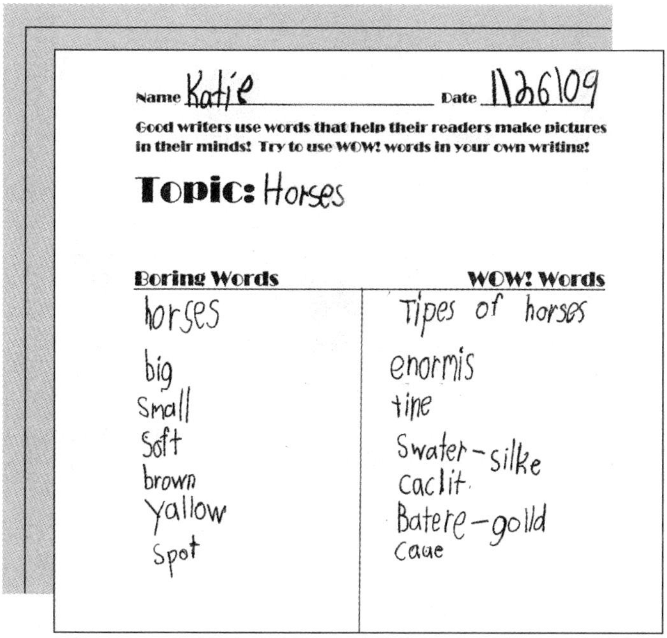

Name Katie Date 1\26\09

Good writers use words that help their readers make pictures in their minds! Try to use WOW! words in your own writing!

Topic: Horses

Boring Words	WOW! Words
horses	Tipes of horses
big	enormis
Small	tine
Soft	Swater-silke
brown	caclit
yallow	Batere-golld
spot	caue

Katie's wow word think sheet

12. Nonfiction Writing: Other Craft Lessons

Writing is a craft, not an art.

~ *William Zinsser*

Speaking Directly to the Reader

Jen began, "I've noticed that many nonfiction authors do something very interesting when they write. They talk to the reader as if the author were right in the room with us. Listen to Joanne Oppenheim's *Have You Seen Bugs?*"

Resource Materials

- ✓ Nonfiction books to demonstrate craft: speaking directly to the reader and question-and-answer format

Have you seen bugs?
Have you seen bugs
and how they move?

"The author is talking right to us, and she does this by using the word 'you': 'Have *you* seen bugs?'

"Today, when you go back to write, think about which way you want to write: talking to the reader or talking from 'I.'

"Here is Jack's piece in which he talks to the reader" (see Figure 3.10).

Figure 3.10

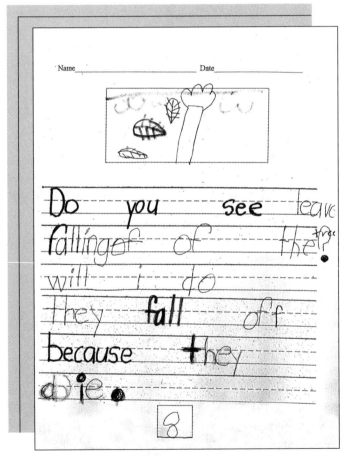

Jack talks to the reader in his piece on leaves.

Question and Answer

"Writers," Jen continued, "today I want to talk to you about one way nonfiction authors write, and we've talked about this a little bit already. I've noticed that many nonfiction authors start with a question and then answer it. Then they ask another question, and they answer that one. Let me give you an example from *Have You Seen Bugs?* The author starts with a question, 'Have you seen bugs?' Then she spends the next three or four pages answering her question: 'Itty-bitty bugs . . . wide-winged bugs . . . bugs with stripes/or speckles/or spots.'

"Next, she asks another question, 'Have you seen bugs and how they move?' She answers by describing different ways bugs move: 'Long-legged bugs/jumping with a bound,/short-legged bugs/running on the ground.'

"She keeps on asking questions and then answering them in the book."

Reading Workshop Research

During reading workshop, before writing workshop, children spent about fifteen to twenty minutes reading about their topics. We selected appropriate books, magazine, or Internet Web site pages on their topics, and as they were reading, if they discovered something new that they might want to add to their piece, they placed a sticky note with an exclamation point on the page. With their reading partners, they shared the new information they learned. During writing workshop, they added their new information to their pieces. Jen suggested that they not open their books while they were adding to their pieces but to remember the information they told their partners.

---

13. Nonfiction Writing: Elaboration

To be clear is the first duty of a writer.

~ *Brander Matthews*

"Writers," Jen began, "you have been working so hard to create fact-filled and interesting nonfiction books. Readers are going to be so excited to read your books and learn from you. Today, I am going to show you something that professional writers do to help make their writing better.

Resource Materials

✓ Blank chart and easel

"First, you read your piece out loud, and if you get to a sentence that sounds a little confusing, or you think you can say a little more, stop and think. Hmm. What is it that I am trying to teach my reader? And, what else can I say about this?

"We've been working on a book together about hermit crabs. I am going to read the section we wrote called 'How Do Hermit Crabs Move?' 'Sometimes hermit crabs move slowly, and sometimes hermit crabs move fast.'

"Hmm. I am thinking that it might be hard for readers to have a good picture in their minds of what we mean. Okay, how about this, 'Sometimes hermit crabs move as slow as a turtle and sometimes hermit crabs move as fast as a jack rabbit running from an enemy.' I think that my new sentences will be more interesting to the reader and help our reader picture how fast and slow the hermit crab really can go. This is what writers do; they find a spot in their piece where they have more to say, and then they think about what other details they could add, and add that to their writing. One way you can add the new part is by writing it on this long strip of paper and then taping it to the side of the piece where you think the information should go.

"Okay, writers, so now it is your turn. Pull out your nonfiction pieces, and look for a spot where you feel like you have more to say and can add more details. Once you find it, underline it." We gave students time to do this work.

Jen said, "So writers, when you go back to your seats, your job is to look at the sentence that you underlined. Get a new sheet of paper, and add more to that part of your piece. If you need more room, you can get a new strip of paper and tape it to your original piece right next to the spot where the new words should go."

Jen's Reflection

Most nonfiction writing elaboration consists of researching, finding more details, and adding information. Some of the elaboration came after I gave the mini-lesson on adding wow words and during one-on-one conferences. Tommy, who was writing about tigers, initially wrote in his piece that tigers "live in the zoo," but after reading a Zoobooks *magazine about tigers, he elaborated and added "and in the jungle."*

14. Nonfiction Writing: Diagrams

Detail makes the difference between boring and terrific writing.

~ Rhys Alexander

We waited until the first graders were almost finished with their writing and research before introducing diagrams or any detailed sketching or drawing. We learned from experience that many young writers will choose to spend all their time drawing diagrams in minute detail and won't write any words at all.

> **Resource Materials**
>
> ✓ *Apples* by Gail Gibbons or other nonfiction books with diagrams
> ✓ Children's completed table of contents pages

Jen told the kids as they gathered for writing workshop, "As you were writing, I looked over my table of contents and noticed that we could have a chapter called 'Parts of a Hermit Crab,' and I started to wonder whether a chapter had to be filled with *all* writing. I realized that I could make this chapter clearer for my reader by using a diagram rather than writing out and trying to describe all the parts of a hermit crab. So, today, we're going to learn to recognize when to use a diagram, and I'm going to show you how to make one in case you decide to use one in your nonfiction books."

Jen explained to the kids that a diagram is like a labeled picture and then continued on with the lesson plan.

"When I thought about describing all of the parts of a hermit crab, I noticed right away what a challenge it would be to write all the words needed to describe the parts of a hermit crab and to create a picture in my readers' minds. I thought, 'Why not just draw a picture?' So I decided to look at Gail Gibbons's book *Apples* to see whether she had done something like that. Look," Jen said, as she held up the book for the class to see, "here is a diagram, or a labeled picture, in one of her books, and we're going to try to do the same thing with our topic." Jen had made a diagram beforehand and held it up alongside the one in Gibbons's book. "Look. Here I've labeled all of the most important parts of a hermit crab.

Alexandra creates a "Different Types of Dogs" page for her expert book.

"So, do you see how I chose a topic from my table of contents, decided it would be easier for my readers to understand it if I used a diagram, selected the correct paper, and then got to work?

"Writers, today I want you to review your table of contents. Look to see whether you have a big idea that might work better as a diagram. If you do, great. If not, maybe you could add one." Jen asked them to take out their table of contents and read them quietly as they sat on the rug. She asked for thumbs up if they had a good topic for a diagram. A show of thumbs went up and a few of the kids shared their ideas. Speaking mostly to the kids who hadn't shown thumbs up, she asked whether any of their peers' thoughts had spurred ideas for diagrams of their own. A few more thumbs went up this time, and again, they shared some of these ideas.

"Writers, I think you're all ready to go off and create your diagrams.

"Remember, as you write today, think, 'Would this information be better if I wrote it out or if I created a diagram?' 'How will my readers be able to best understand what I am trying to teach them?'"

Figure 3.11 shows Katie's diagram of a horse.

Figure 3.11

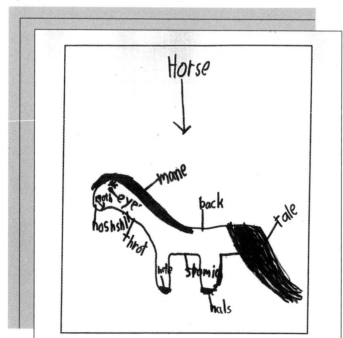

Katie's diagram of the parts of a horse

Jen's Reflection

Gather a few nonfiction books that include diagrams. We used Apples by Gail Gibbons and Surprising Sharks by Nicola Davies, but there are many others. Show kids why authors use diagrams and what kind of information they are meant to convey. Not everyone will have the need for a diagram, but most will be eager to try this popular nonfiction device.

Other Features of Nonfiction Writing

- Index
- Glossary
- Photographs and captions
- Pronunciation key

15. Writing Partner Revision

A writer is, after all, only half of his book.
The other half is the reader and from the reader the writer learns.

~ *P.L. Travers*

Once the nonfiction books were well under way, we gave a mini-lesson on the writing partner revision strategy. We asked the kids to share only their table of contents with their writing partner and to ask their partners, "What do you wonder about my

Resource Materials

✓ Writing partners

topic?" Their partner wrote their wonder on a sticky note and read the piece to see whether it was answered in the text. If so, their partner gave them a compliment and then they switched. If the wonder was not answered in the text, the author had a decision to make. If authors felt that their partner's question was important to include, they went back to add that information to the piece. But, if they felt that the wonder wouldn't necessarily improve their piece, they had the choice, of course, not to revise. Many of the children chose to add to their pieces since we had focused on audience and the kind of information the reader wanted to know. If the partner's question couldn't be added without research, we helped them locate the information in their books.

Ryan discusses his writing progress with Trinity as he decides on the next step to take.

Jen's Reflection

This lesson pushed the kids' thinking a little further and got them to think of their readers. After the authors revised their writing, they got back together with their partners and read them the added information.

16. Editing: Using Word Wall Words

Clutter is the disease of American writing. We are a society strangling in unnecessary words, circular constructions, pompous frills and meaningless jargon.

~ William Zinsser

Jen began the mini-lesson. "Now that we've almost finished our nonfiction pieces, we're going to begin to look at our pieces for capitals, periods, and spelling. It's called editing our pieces, and all writers need to do this before they can say that their writing is finished.

"Today, we are all going to become word wall detectives. The word wall words are words that we should know in a snap, and they are also on the word wall, so they follow the rule, 'When in sight, spell it right!' Your partner is going to be able to help you with this today. Watch closely as I become a word wall detective for my own writing first, and then I will ask my partner to help me." Jen took out a piece with some word wall words spelled incorrectly. "Okay, here I go. I reread my piece, touching each word and asking myself, is this a word wall word? When I come to a word wall word that doesn't seem right, I circle it. Okay, now I'm going to fix these words. Either find the word on the word wall, or use patterns in the word wall to help you with other words.

"Now, it is your turn to help. You all will be my partner. Let's reread my writing, and see if you can be word wall detectives for me. See if I missed any word wall words that aren't spelled right. Read it over and tell me what you think. When you have found one put your thumb up. Turn and tell your partner what I could do. Great, I fixed that up. Thanks for helping me be a better writer.

"Remember what I did. I didn't wait for my partner to check my work first. I was a word wall detective myself and checked my work, and then I asked for help. Try to spell the words correctly the first time. But if you forget, that's what going back and fixing up your work is about, and having a partner who can help you is a great thing!"

Jen then handed out purple pens to the children. "Writers, it's time to finish up your writing for today. Each of you, take a few minutes to edit your writing. Make sure each sentence has a capital and punctuation, and then look at your words to see if you spelled them correctly. Circle the words you're not sure about. Look around the room and on the word wall to see if it's in sight, and then spell it correctly.

Resource Materials

✓ Easy to Read Writing editing checklist (*see Appendix*)

✓ Purple pens

"Now quickly and quietly get with your partner. Have your partner read it with you. Your partner can help you circle any other words that may need to be fixed up. Then give the story back to the writer, and give the writer a second chance to fix up their work."

17. Partner Editing: Capitals and Periods

Writing is edit, edit, edit.

~ *William Zinsser*

Resource Materials

✓ Easy to Read Writing editing checklist (*see Appendix*)

✓ Blue pen

"Writing partners can really help one another when they write," said Jen. "Today, I am going to teach you that you can use your partner to help you check for capitals and periods.

"Writers, one way to help your partner find good places for a period is for one partner to just read his or her piece while the other partner listens carefully for places where the writer pauses. When you hear the writer pause, you need to make a clicking noise with your mouth. Like this. Then the writer checks for a period followed by a capital letter. Watch and listen while you help me check my piece for capitals and periods.

"I need your help. I want you to pretend that you are my partner and you are going to help me find where I need capitals and periods in my piece. I will read it to you, and you will click when you hear me pause. Then, I will add my period if I need one and check for a capital letter. Ready?

"So, writers, today and every day when we are working on a piece, we can use partners to help us make our pieces better and easier to read. Partners, ready?"

For the share time, after the partner told the writer where he or she might add a capital letter or a period (using a blue pen, which was handed out to the class as a special "editing" pen), students walked around and looked at their friends' pieces for places they used blue pen to add capitals and periods.

Jen's Reflection

The editing work the kids did on their nonfiction pieces was a continuation of editing they had been engaged in with personal narrative. We gave them an editing checklist titled Easy to Read Writing (see Appendix) that reminded them what editing they were responsible for. The editing for punctuation was based on Teaching the Youngest Writers: A Practical Guide *by Marcia Freeman (1998), a great resource for writing teachers.*

Assessment Rubric for Nonfiction Writing

I use the following rubric during conferring time with my students to help guide me in planning small groups and conferences. I put one slash in a column when I have modeled the strategy for a child—either one-on-one or in a small group—and then make it into an X once I see the child using the skill a few times on his or her own. These are skills that are taught in whole group, but we know that most young children need to have the skills modeled for them a few times before they will give them a try on their own. This system helps me keep track of which students might need to have the strategy reinforced and lets me know at a quick glance the strategies that are being used consistently so I can move on to something else. It is also a quick and easy way for me to gather information for report cards. In addition, this rubric has been a nice way for me to focus on the unit and remind myself what is most important for the students to take away with them.

QUALITIES OF GOOD WRITING

STUDENT NAME	Grammar/Mechanics • Caps/periods • Word wall words • Spaces	Used two to three nonfiction features: table of contents, glossary, index, diagram, captions	Craft/Revision • Elaboration • Used two to three sentences on a page • Interesting beginning • Used "I" or "you" • Changed one word for a better word	Structure and Focus • Used table of contents to structure piece • Piece is all about one topic • Used planning sheet • Chapters are in order	Independence/Stamina • Came up with topic using wonders

18. Publishing and Celebrating

*The beauty of the written word is that it can be held close to the heart
and read over and over again.*

~ *Florence Littauer*

We had worked hard, written, and read much, so now it was time to celebrate. Students had become teachers of their knowledge and the experts of their topics in our classroom. We decided to celebrate by having the first graders teach the kindergarten students what they had learned about their topics. The kindergartners were thrilled to come and listen to what the first graders had learned.

Resource Materials

✓ Family letter
(see Appendix)

✓ Another class of students

After they had finished creating covers, writing dedication pages, and writing a book blurb on the back of their books, the first graders were ready to share. Jen invited the kindergarten students into the classroom, and you could feel the excitement. The first graders were bursting to share their new knowledge. We paired the students up, and the first graders invited their kindergarten partners to their writing space to read their nonfiction books aloud. Before they began reading to the kindergartners, Jen instructed the authors to read aloud the title and chapters in the table of contents. They asked the kindergartners, "What do you expect to learn?" The kindergartners shared their thoughts and the reading began. At the end, as the kids were finishing up their books, Jen and the kindergarten teacher walked around to the groups, asking the kindergartners what they learned today. Jen's first graders burst with pride as the kindergartners shared the many facts they had learned.

That day, Jen's students felt like true authors and illustrators and realized that they had a lot of knowledge to teach others.

Jen's Reflection

We included the children's nonfiction books in the class library for others to read and continue to learn from (see Figure 3.12 for an example). We also sent a letter home with the nonfiction books attached (also in Appendix).

Dear Families,

We are pleased to let you know that the children have just finished another unit of study in writing. The children have been studying elements of nonfiction work in both reading and writing workshop.

Our writers have learned to use read-and-write elements such as: tables of contents, indexes, glossaries, wow words, and many others. We read many authors of nonfiction writing to help mentor us in this work and also thought about our questions and wonders on our topics to make our pieces unique.

Attached is a draft of one nonfiction piece your child has written. Your child also has a published piece that is being celebrated in the classroom. Please look over the writing work for the elements listed above and feel free to come in and see your child's published nonfiction book. Help your child celebrate all that he or she has learned as a reader, writer, and wonderer!

The children's published nonfiction books became their favorite reading material during independent reading time. Their books also were an important reference tool for other classes engaged in a nonfiction study.

Conclusion

We noticed that as the children became actively engaged in the wonder centers and explored writing nonfiction, their questions inspired more questions, their observations led to more curiosity and discoveries, and their seeking answers to questions led to a renewed confidence in knowing how to explore explanations. For the students in Jen's class, the world of school became a place of exploration and wonder.

As the wise woman tells a child in *The Wise Woman and Her Secret* (Merriam 1999), "The secret of wisdom is to be curious—to take the time to look closely, to use all your senses to see and touch and taste and smell and hear. To keep on wondering."

Our hopes for the students in Jen's class, and for all young children, are similar to the wise woman's: to maintain a sense of wonder, to be hungry to explore the world, and to keep asking questions about everything they're learning in school and in their lives. We believe that as children grow, they will keep that curiosity and passion, and they will flourish into aware and inquisitive adults.

Figure 3.12

Sam's finished nonfiction book on snow

Figure 3.12 (continued)

Chapter 2. How to make snowmen and snowgirls?

Do you know how to make snowmen and snowgirls? Well You will learn today. Look on the picture then you will no. Now do you no now!

How to make snowmen

1. Make 3 snowballs. Make a giant one a medium one and a small one.

2. Add stuff add sticks for arms. A hat, A carrot and buttons and a scarf.

3. Make shore You are correct.

4. You are done.

Chapter 3. Things to do in snow?

What do you want to do in snow? You can snow bord and gosled riding or make a snowmen. Do what you want.

I like to make snowmen.

igure 3.12 (continued)

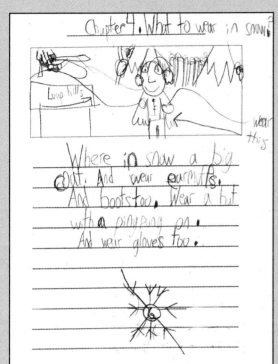

Chapter 4. What to wear in snow?

wear this

Where in snow a big coat. And wear earmuffs. And boots too. Wear a hat with a pingpong on. And wear gloves too.

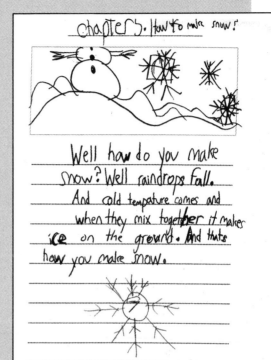

Chapter 5. How to make snow?

Well how do you make snow? Well raindrops fall. And cold tempature comes and when they mix together it makes ice on the ground. And thats how you make snow.

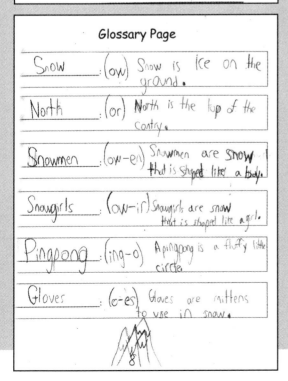

Glossary Page

Snow	(ow)	Snow is ice on the ground.
North	(or)	North is the top of the contry.
Snowmen	(ow-en)	Snowmen are snow that is shaped like a body.
Snowgirls	(ow-ir)	Snowgirls are snow that is shaped like a girl.
Pingpong	(ing-o)	A pingpong is a fluffy little circle.
Gloves	(o-es)	Gloves are mittens to use in snow.

Thank you for reading this book.

Books for Nonfiction Research
Wonder Writing

Avison, Brigid. 2003. *I Wonder Why I Blink: And Other Questions About My Body*. Boston: Kingfisher.

Berger, Melvin A. 2002. *Why Do Volcanoes Blow Their Tops? Questions and Answers About Volcanoes and Earthquakes*. Beijing, China: People's Literature Publishing.

Branley, Franklyn M. 1996. *What Makes a Magnet?* Let's-Read-and-Find-Out Science series, Stage 2. New York: HarperCollins.

Brocklehurst, Ruth. 2004. *Children's Picture Atlas*. Tulsa, OK: Usborne Books.

This picture atlas takes young readers on a visual journey around the world.

Charman, Andrew. 2003. *I Wonder Why Trees Have Leaves: And Other Questions About Plants*. Boston: Kingfisher.

Christelow, Eileen. 1992. *What Do Authors Do?* North Port, FL: Sandpiper Press.

Davies, Nicola. 2008. *Surprising Sharks*. Cambridge, MA: Candlewick.

Ganeri, Anita. 2003. *I Wonder Why the Sea Is Salty: And Other Questions About the Oceans*. Boston: Kingfisher.

———. 2003. *I Wonder Why the Wind Blows: And Other Questions About Our Planet*. Boston: Kingfisher.

Gibbons, Gail. 2000. *Apples*. New York: Holiday House.

———. 2002. *The Pumpkin Book*. Pine Plains, NY: Live Oak Media.

Heard, Georgia. 1992. *Creatures of Earth, Sea, and Sky*. Honesdale, PA: Boyds Mills Press.

Maynard, Christopher. 2003. *I Wonder Why Planes Have Wings: And Other Questions About Transportation*. Boston: Kingfisher.

Nelson, Robin. 2003. *What Is Water?* Minneapolis, MN: Lerner.

O'Neill, Amanda. 2003. *I Wonder Why Spiders Spin Webs: And Other Questions About Creepy-Crawlies*. Boston: Kingfisher.

———. 2003. *I Wonder Why Snakes Shed Their Skin: And Other Questions About Reptiles*. Boston: Kingfisher.

Oppenheim, Joanne. 1998. *Have You Seen Bugs?* New York: Scholastic.

Ripley, Catherine. 1996. *Why Do Stars Twinkle? And Other Nighttime Questions*. Toronto: Maple Tree Press.

———. 2004. *Why? The Best Ever Question and Answer Book About Nature, Science, and the World Around You*. Toronto: Maple Tree Press.

Santrey, Laurence. 1982. *What Makes the Wind?* New York: Troll Communications.

Strong, Mark. 2004. *Diving Deep*. De Soto, TX: Wright Group/McGraw-Hill.

Taylor, Barbara. 2002. *I Wonder Why Soap Makes Bubbles: And Other Questions About Science*. Boston: Kingfisher.

————. 2003. *I Wonder Why Zippers Have Teeth: And Other Questions About Inventions*. Boston: Kingfisher.

————. 2006. *I Wonder Why the Sun Rises: And Other Questions About Time and Seasons*. Boston: Kingfisher.

Wood, Lily. 2001. *Volcanoes*. New York: Scholastic Reference.

Book Series

HarperCollins: Let's-Read-and-Find-Out Science: Stages 1 & 2

Sample titles include:

Bugs Are Insects

From Caterpillar to Butterfly

From Seed to Pumpkin

From Tadpole to Frog

Scholastic Question and Answer Series

Sample titles include:

Do Tarantulas Have Teeth?

Can Snakes Crawl Backwards?

Can It Rain Cats and Dogs?

Appendix

Dear Wonderers,

We will be turning our classroom into a place of wonder. A place to: observe, ask questions, and study the natural world. This is one way we become inspired to write! Please bring in a beloved object of nature — an acorn, a shell, a nest, a bone, a shark's tooth, a piece of pine, a flower — that you've chosen because you think it is beautiful, it makes you wonder, or it amazes you. We will use these items to create a discovery center where we will observe, question, and appreciate one another's natural treasures. Take your time to choose something really special to you and bring it in to share! We look forward to finding out what inspires you! Please bring your item in by _____.

Love,

[Teacher's Name]

Name_____   Date_____

Discovery Table Observation

Name_____   Date_____

Discovery Table

My Object _____

Draw Your Object	List Words to Describe
I Wonder About . . .	It Reminds Me of . . .

Name_____   Date_____

My Wonders

1.

2.

3.

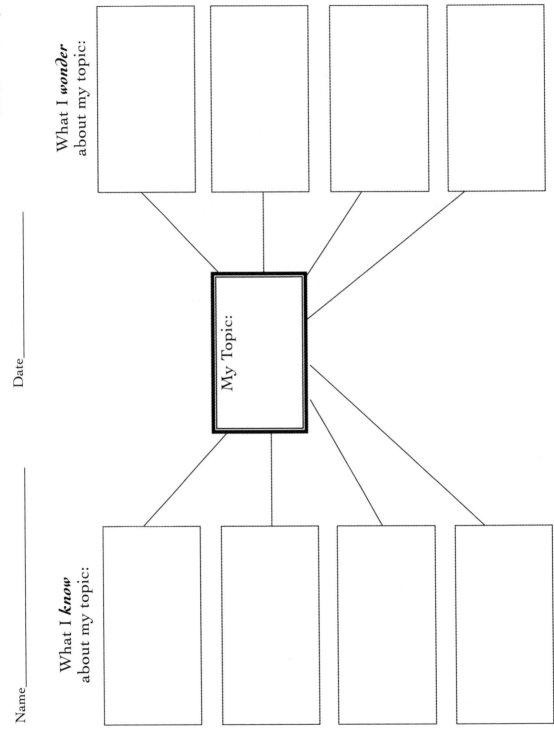

Date_____

Name_____

What I **wonder** about my topic:

My Topic:

What I **know** about my topic:

A Place for Wonder: Reading and Writing Nonfiction in the Primary Grades
by Georgia Heard and Jennifer McDonough. Copyright © 2009. Stenhouse Publishers.

Name_____   Date_____

Table of Contents

_____   _____

(chapter title)   (page number)

_____   _____

(chapter title)   (page number)

_____   _____

(chapter title)   (page number)

_____   _____

(chapter title)   (page number)

_____   _____

(chapter title)   (page number)

_____   _____

(chapter title)   (page number)

Name_____   Date_____

Chapter Paper

Dear Families,

Over the coming weeks, your child will be exploring questions and wonders that he or she has about the world and how it works. Your child would like to explore the following question:

_____

One way we are teaching our young writers to research questions is to interview other people and find out what they know about the topic. Please help your child answer his or her question by answering it yourself or calling on a friend or family member who may be more of an "expert" on the topic. Please help your child write and/or draw what he or she learns on the back of this sheet and return it tomorrow. They will be using this information to help them write a nonfiction book based on their question.

Thanks for your help and support!

Name_____   Date_____

Good writers use words that help their readers make pictures in their minds! Try to use WOW! words in your own writing!

Topic:

Boring Words	WOW! Words

Easy to Read Writing

Did I...

___ sketch and label?

___ stretch out the sounds in the word?

___ put spaces in between words?

Ilikemycat.	I like my cat.

___ use word wall words?

a	do	get	like
out	put	the	with

___ start my sentence with a capital letter?

i like my cat.	I like my cat.

___ use a period at the end of a sentence?

I like my cat	I like my cat.

Dear Families,

We are pleased to let you know that the children have just finished another unit of study in writing. The children have been studying elements of nonfiction work in both reading and writing workshop.

Our writers have learned to use read-and-write elements such as: tables of contents, indexes, glossaries, wow words, and many others. We read many authors of nonfiction writing to help mentor us in this work and also thought about our questions and wonders on our topics to make our pieces unique.

Attached is a draft of one nonfiction piece your child has written. Your child also has a published piece that is being celebrated in the classroom. Please look over the writing work for the elements listed above and feel free to come in and see your child's published nonfiction book. Help your child celebrate all that he or she has learned as a reader, writer, and wonderer!

Straight Lines

All the kindergartners
walk to recess and back
in a perfectly straight line
no words between them.
They must stifle their small voices,
their laughter, they must
stop the little skip in their walk,
they must not dance or hop
or run or exclaim.
They must line up
at the water fountain
straight, and in perfect form,
like the brick wall behind them.
One of their own given the job
of informer — guard of quiet,
soldier of stillness.
If they talk
or make a sound
they will lose their stars.
Little soldiers marching to and from
pretend
their hair sweaty
from escaping dinosaurs
their hearts full of loving the world
and all they want to do
is shout it out
at the top of their lungs.
When they walk back to class
they must quietly
fold their pretends into pockets,
must dam the river of words,
ones they're just learning
new words that hold the power
to light the skies, and if they don't
a star is taken away.
One star
by one star
until night grows dark and heavy
while they learn to think carefully
before skipping,
before making a wish.

A Place for Wonder: Reading and Writing Nonfiction in the Primary Grades
by Georgia Heard and Jennifer McDonough. Copyright © 2009. Stenhouse Publishers.

Resources

Barry, Frances. 2008. *Little Green Frogs*. Boston: Candlewick Press.

Baylor, Byrd. 1997. *The Other Way to Listen*. New York: Aladdin.

Bayrock, Fiona. 2009. *Bubble Homes and Fish Farts*. Watertown, MA: Charlesbridge.

Bishop, Nic. 2008. *Nic Bishop Frogs*. New York: Scholastic Nonfiction.

———. 2008. *Nic Bishop Spiders*. New York: Scholastic Nonfiction.

Campbell, Sarah C. 2008. *Wolfsnail: A Backyard Predator*. Honesdale, PA: Boyds Mills Press.

Curtis, J. L. 2000. *Where Do Balloons Go?* New York: Joanna Cotler Books.

Early, Jo Ann. 2008. *Flip, Float, Fly! Seeds on the Move*. New York: Holiday House.

Franco, Betsy. 2008. *Bees, Snails, & Peacock Tails: Patterns & Shapes . . . Naturally*. New York: Margaret K. McElderry Books.

Holub, Joan. 2001. *Why Do Dogs Bark?* New York: Puffin Books.

———. 2003. *Why Do Horses Neigh?* New York: Scholastic.

Hopkins, Lee Bennett, ed. 1994. *Questions: Poems of Wonder*. New York: HarperTrophy.

———. 2009. *Sky Magic*. New York: Dutton's Children's Books.

Hulbert, Jay, and Sid Kantor. 1990. *Armando Asked, "Why?"* Portsmouth, NH: Heinemann Library.

Jenkins, Steve. *Sisters and Brothers: Sibling Relationships in the Animal World.* Boston: Houghton Mifflin Books for Children.

Melmed, Laura Krauss. 1993. *The First Song Ever Sung.* New York: Lothrop Lee & Shepard.

Merriam, Eve. 1999. *The Wise Woman and Her Secret.* New York: Aladdin.

Oppenheim, Joanne. 1998. *Have You Seen Bugs?* New York: Scholastic.

Ripley, Catherine. 2001. *Why?* Toronto: Maple Tree Press.

Seeger, Laura Vaccaro. 2007. *First the Egg.* New York: Roaring Brook Press.

Serafini, Frank. 2008. Looking Closely Inside series (*The Forest, The Shore, The Desert, The Garden*). Tonawanda, NY: Kids Can Press.

Showers, Paul. 1993. *The Listening Walk.* New York: HarperCollins.

Silver, Donald. 1993. *One Small Square: Backyard.* New York: Learning Triangle Press.

Singer, Marilyn. 2008. *Eggs.* New York: Holiday House.

I Wonder Why Series

Avison, Brigid 2003. *I Wonder Why I Blink: And Other Questions About My Body*. Boston: Kingfisher.

Dunbar, Joyce, and James Dunbar. 1991. *Why Is the Sky Up?* Boston: Houghton Mifflin.

Ganeri, Anita. 2003. *I Wonder Why the Sea Is Salty: And Other Questions About the Oceans*. Boston: Kingfisher.

Lobb, Janice. 2001. *Counting Sheep: Why Do We Sleep?* Boston: Kingfisher.

Maynard, Christopher. 2003. *I Wonder Why Planes Have Wings: And Other Questions About Transportation*. Boston: Kingfisher.

Stott, Carole. 2003. *I Wonder Why Stars Twinkle: And Other Questions About Space*. Boston: Kingfisher.

Taylor, Barbara. 1994. *I Wonder Why Soap Makes Bubbles: And Other Questions About Science*. Boston: Kingfisher.

———. 1997. *I Wonder Why the Sun Rises: And Other Questions About Time and Seasons*. Boston: Kingfisher.

———. 2001. *I Wonder Why Zippers Have Teeth: And Other Questions About Inventions*. Boston: Kingfisher.

Magazines

Click: a science and exploration magazine designed for children aged 3–7 (K–2). www.cobblestonepub.com.

National Geographic Young Explorer (K–1). www.kids.nationalgeographic.com.

Zoobooks: the animal magazine for kids. www.zoobooks.com.

Web Sites and Blogs

Web Sites

Children & Nature Network: Building a Movement to Reconnect Children & Nature. www.childrenandnature.org.

This Web site and movement was inspired by Richard Louv's book *The Last Child in the Woods: Saving Our Children from Nature-Deficit Disorder*, and was created to support a national network of people and organizations that encourage children to reconnect to nature.

Discovery Education Streaming Plus. www.discoveryeducation.com/products/streaming.

Large high-quality video library, with more than 9,000 titles.

Project Learning Tree. www.plt.org.

According to the Web site, Project Learning Tree is "an award-winning environmental education program" created for teachers of grades pre-K–12.

Project WILD. www.projectwild.org.

According to the Web site, Project WILD is "a wildlife-focused conservation education program for K–12 educators and their students."

Blogs

Bloggers across the "kidlitosphere" celebrate nonfiction Monday by writing about nonfiction books for kids every Monday. These blogs are usually run by teachers, and they are an invaluable resource. If you check out one blog, it will link to many others. Here are just a few of our favorites:

A Year of Reading. www.readingyear.blogspot.com.

Wild About Nature. www.wildaboutnaturewriters.blogspot.com.

SimplyScience Blog. www.simplyscience.wordpress.com.

Chicken Spaghetti. www.chickenspaghetti.typepad.com.

The Miss Rumphius Effect. www.missrumphiuseffect.blogspot.com.

Interesting Nonfiction for Kids. www.inkrethink.blogspot.com.

Bibliography

Bender, Sue. 1991. *Plain and Simple: A Woman's Journey into the Amish*. New York: HarperOne.

Broda, Herbert W. 2007. *Schoolyard-Enhanced Learning: Using the Outdoors as an Instructional Tool, K–8*. Portland, ME: Stenhouse.

Calkins, Lucy. 2003. *The Units of Study for Primary Writing: A Yearlong Curriculum Series*. Portsmouth, NH: Heinemann.

Carson, Rachel. 1965. *The Sense of Wonder*. New York: HarperCollins.

Chittenden, Edward, and Jacqueline Jones. 1999. "Science Assessment in Early Childhood Programs." American Association for the Advancement of Science. http://www.project2061.org/publications/earlychild/online/experience/cjones.htm.

Collins, Kathy. 2004. *Growing Readers: Units of Study in the Primary Classroom*. Portland, ME: Stenhouse.

Cott, Jonathan. 1996. *Thirteen: A Journey into the Number*. New York: Doubleday.

Donadio, Rachel. 2005. "Every Day Is All There Is." *New York Times*, October 9. Available from http://www.nytimes.com/2005/10/09/books/review/09donadio.html?pagewanted=print.

Ferra, Lorraine. 1994. *A Crow Doesn't Need a Shadow: A Guide to Writing Poetry from Nature*. Layton, UT: Gibbs Smith.

Fox, Matthew. 1995. *The Reinvention of Work: A New Vision of Livelihood for Our Time*. New York: HarperCollins.

Freeman, Marcia. 1998. *Teaching the Youngest Writers: A Practical Guide.* Gainsville, FL: Maupin Press.

Harwayne, Shelley. 2005. *Novel Perspectives.* Portsmouth, NH: Heinemann.

Heard, Georgia. 1992. *Creatures of Earth, Sea, and Sky: Animal Poems.* Honesdale, PA: Boyds Mills Press.

————. 2002. *The Revision Toolbox: Teaching Techniques That Work.* Portsmouth, NH: Heinemann.

Hinchman, Hannah. 1997. *A Trail Through Leaves: The Journal as a Path to Place.* New York: W. W. Norton.

Jones, Jill A. 2006. "Student-Involved Classroom Libraries." *The Reading Teacher* 59(6): 576–580.

Lear, Linda J. 2007. *Beatrix Potter: A Life in Nature.* New York: St. Martin's.

Louv, Richard. 2008. *The Last Child in the Woods: Saving Our Children from Nature Deficit Disorder.* Chapel Hill, NC: Algonquin Books.

Macaulay, David. 1988. *The Way Things Work.* Boston: Houghton Mifflin.

McPhee, John. 1966. *Oranges.* New York: Farrar, Straus and Giroux.

Miller, Debbie. 2002. *Reading with Meaning: Teaching Comprehension in the Primary Grades.* Portland, ME: Stenhouse.

Pennsylvania Department of Education and Department of Public Welfare. 2007. *Pennsylvania Learning Standards for Early Childhood*. Harrisburg, PA: Pennsylvania Department of Education.

Sobel, David T. 2008. *Childhood and Nature: Design Principles for Educators*. Portland, ME: Stenhouse.

Thomas, Lewis. 1983. *Late Night Thoughts on Listening to Mahler's Ninth Symphony*. New York: Bantam Books.

Wieseltier, Leon. 2004. "Translation; Yehuda Amichai: Posthumous Fragments." *New York Times*, November 21. Available from http://query.nytimes.com/gst/fullpage.html?res=9B06E1DE1F3CF932A15752C1A9629C8B63&fta=y.

If you found *A Place for Wonder* by Georgia Heard and Jennifer McDonough to be helpful for your professional development, we think you would enjoy these other Stenhouse titles.

The Castle in the Classroom
Story as a Springboard for Early Literacy
Ranu Bhattacharyya
Foreword by Georgia Heard

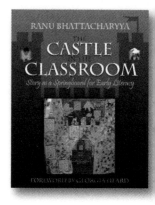

The Castle in the Classroom describes a year in a kindergarten classroom as the children embark on literary exploration. The detailed focus lessons throughout the book use the power of stories to deepen the literary experience so that reading and writing become as much a part of kindergarten as playing and pretending.

Grades Pre-K–2 • 2010 • 168 pages • CS-0770 • $19.00 paper

Praise for *The Castle in the Classroom*

"Here is my wish for all young children—that they too can experience a class as inspiring as Ranu's. Here is my wish for all teachers—when you read The Castle in the Classroom, *let Ranu's wise teaching be your guide."* — Georgia Heard

[The Castle in the Classroom] *is one of those rare professional books that truly captures the joy of teaching."* — Bonnie Hill Campbell

"An excellent survey, filled with inviting perspectives on reading to a diverse audience." — *The Midwest Book Review*, February 2011

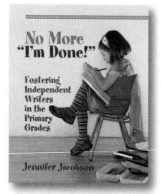

No More "I'm Done!"
Fostering Independent Writers in the Primary Grades
Jennifer Jacobson

No More "I'm Done!" demonstrates how to create a more productive, engaging, and rewarding writing workshop that helps nurture independent, self-directed writers. Jennifer Jacobson guides teachers from creating a supportive classroom environment through establishing effective routines, shows how to set up a writing workshop, and provides an entire year of devel¬opmentally appropriate mini-lessons.

Grades K–2 • 2010 • 176 pages • CS-0784 • $19.00 paper

Praise for *No More "I'm Done!"*

"[No More "I'm Done!"] *is nothing short of an intense professional development package."* — *Education Review*, June 2010

"This was a great book! The author described in detail each part of the ideal writing workshop and how to foster independence through words and actions." — Goodreads.com, July 2011

"I never thought a teaching book could inspire me to work on my own writing skills but this one has. Every teacher who has struggled with teaching children how to write should read this book. Jennifer Jacobson has hit the nail on the head with this one." — Mrs. Brown's Grade 2 Blog, July 2011

For more information or to preview sample chapters from these and other titles, visit www.stenhouse.com